The Wine Companion

A congenial guide to
wines, spirits and liqueurs

David Burroughs and Norman Bezzant

Collins

Glasgow and London

First published 1975
Published by William Collins Sons and Company Limited,
Glasgow and London

Copyright © The Wine and Spirit Education Trust Limited 1975

Maps and tables by Reg Piggott
Line drawings by Virginia Smith

'Gin Lane' etching reproduced by permission of Mary Evans
Picture Library

Colour illustrations by courtesy of:

British Museum (Ancient Egyptian Amphora)
British Tourist Authority (Exterior, Oasthouses)
Bureau National de Cognac (Cognac Pot Still)
Comité Interprofessionel du Vin de Champagne (Casks in Champagne
    Chai; Champagne Press after the first crushing of the grapes)
Food from France (Soil: Champagne region; Clos-de-Vougeot and
    its Château in Burgundy)
Ronald D. Oakes, Highland Distilleries (Bunnahabhain Distillery)
Sherry House Ltd (Still Room of the Benedictine Factory at Fécamp)
W. A. Warre Esq., MW (Soil: Port Region of the Douro Valley)
Wine and Spirit Education Trust (Soil: Bordeaux Region; Soil:
    Châteauneuf-du-Pape, Rhône Region; Vines trained high; Vines
    trained low; A bunch of ripe Riesling grapes; Harvesting the grapes;
    Interior of a typical Off-Licence)

Printed in Great Britain
ISBN 0 00 435217 3

Contents

Colour illustrations

Introduction

by Hugh Johnson

Wine is different from other drinks. It has a background of infinite complexity. The more you enjoy wine the more you want to delve into what lies behind it. Pleasure stimulates interest, and interest increases pleasure. Hence the unending demand for wine books.

I look forward to the new ones as they come out, but rarely do I find so much sound information packed into a manageable compass as in *The Wine Companion*.

The book was conceived to tell the budding wine-merchant about his wares. It succeeds so well that the publisher decided on an edition for the wine-merchant's customers – the wine-loving public.

I heartily recommend it to everyone who takes pleasure in wine.

Authors' Preface

To understand and appreciate wines, spirits, liqueurs and beers, the reader needs to know something of each of the three stages in their lives: firstly, their origins and the sources of their ingredients; secondly, their refinement into bottles bearing any one of a thousand different labels; and thirdly, their selection for various social purposes and their care in the home.

But that is not all: in a rapidly changing world, up-to-date information is a necessity, and recent changes in the world of wines and spirits are quite dramatic. They concern the laws of many countries and the consequent alterations in the description and quality of wines and spirits, development of the wine-maker's skills, and changes in marketing methods, licensing, and of fashion in drinking habits.

To clarify the present situation, we have reviewed the whole field. In this book, the history and geography of wines, spirits and beers have been treated, with short descriptions of life in the vineyard, the winery, the distillery and the brewery. More immediately, there is a wealth of advice to the consumer on tasting, selecting, storing and serving wines and spirits. Appendices, a glossary and pronunciation guide, and an index have been added, with the object of making this book a much-needed work of reference for the wine-lover.

The subjects treated here are numerous; thankfully, we have been able to draw on the experience of experts on each and every one of them. These experts, of the present and the past, have contributed to the knowledge and skills of the Wine and Spirit Education Trust, which is responsible for training in the Wine Trade. We hasten to acknowledge the help received from the Trust's personnel and also from its extensive library in authentication of the text and illustrations of *The Wine Companion*.

The origins and the role of nature

'Wine is the alcoholic beverage obtained from the fermentation of the juice of freshly-gathered grapes, the fermentation taking place in the district of origin according to local tradition and practice.'

This definition gives an excellent starting-point to the story of wine. Very many varieties have been perfected over the centuries, and without doubt wines with new characteristics are yet to be discovered, but to be classed as wines they must all obey the precepts of this definition.

The history of wine-making
The phrases 'district of origin' and 'local tradition and practice' instantly beg the question 'Where and when did it all start?' And although this is a romantic story, it does not begin with 'Once upon a time' quite so much as with 'Here beginneth . . .'. For the art and skill of the wine-maker predate the written record, and it was archaeologists who discovered evidence of wine-making some twelve thousand years ago. When later, Noah is recorded as landing with his ark on Mount Ararat, he planted a vineyard, and was to be reproved by Jehovah for his drunkenness.

Was it such an accident that already man knew the secret of wine production, and its benefits? It will be shown in this book that in the grape, Nature herself provided a most remarkable set of prepacked ingredients in a form exceeding in ingenuity all the skills of the modern food manufacturer. It only remained for man to open the package and mix the ingredients.

And there, under Mount Ararat, on the southern slopes of the Caucasus Mountains, flanked by the Caspian and Black Seas, the cultivation of the vine first flourished. The making of wine

originated in this area, centred on Shiraz in ancient Persia, and
here the poet Omar Khayyam posed the whimsical question: 'I
often wonder what the vintners buy, one half as precious as the
stuff they sell . . .'.

From the Persians the craft spread southwest to Assyria,
south to Babylon, and northwest to the shores of the Black Sea.
The Assyrians made much of the innovation. The Babylonian
king, Nebuchadnezzar, became the owner of vineyards and
wine-cellars. There is even a wine list dating from that time in
existence today. The Assyrians carried the craft down along the
Lebanese coast and beyond to Palestine; and round the Mediterranean elbow to Egypt. Egyptian wall paintings depict the main
stages in the production of wine, with the vines growing on
pergolas or wooden trellises, much as they do today, and show the
grape harvesters using sickle knives identical to those still used
along the Mediterranean coast.

The Psalms of King David of Israel speak often of wine and,
incidentally, of the contemporary economy of the Eastern
Mediterranean. Psalm 104, XV, refers to 'wine that maketh glad
the heart of man, oil to make him of cheerful countenance, and
bread to strengthen man's heart.' In other words, wine, olives
and wheat. And here, already, can be seen a trend which has
persisted through all the centuries down to the present day: the
strong connection between wine and religion.

Next the Phoenicians, the seafarers from Tyre and Sidon in
the Lebanon, took the vine and its secrets along the Mediterranean
shores, and even beyond. Soon the Greeks and the Romans had
the vine and its precious product, and each in turn dedicated a
god to wine. The Greek Dionysus and the Roman Bacchus were
both high-ranking deities.

The Greeks brought wine to the people, when originally it had
been reserved for the lips of kings and gods, and wherever they
set up a colony, from southern France to the Black Sea and from
Sicily to North Africa, the vine came too. Not only did they make
wine locally, but Herodotus tells of exporting wine to Egypt,

while Greek wines from the islands of Chios and Lesbos even challenged the fine wines of Rome in their home city.

The Romans set about the task of wine-making with characteristic thoroughness, and were the first to acclimatize the frost-proof vines extolled by Pliny, planting them in the Bordeaux country, in the valleys of the Rhône, Marne and Seine, and along the Mosel and Rhine. They concentrated their vineyards in these and other selected areas, which were expanded and intensively cultivated. New vineyards were established not only in France but also in Hungary, Germany and England. Vines were planted in England as far north as York, and the Domesday Book records some forty vineyards left by the Romans.

Wherever the Eagle flew the Roman legions brought their own wines, made mostly in Italy and Spain, and where vineyards had previously been planted, as for example in Carthage, they were uprooted and grain crops sown in their place. The Romans embraced Christianity, and when their empire collapsed, the early Christian missionaries carried the vine further north into Europe. They needed sacramental wines, and wherever they built a church they planted a vineyard. Christianity did not outlaw wine, like the Mohammedan religion which followed it; on the contrary, wine was the very life-blood of the Christian faith. When the Romans left England, abandoning it to the Danes and Saxons, it was the church which kept the craft of wine-making alive. Meagre wine supplies came also from Germany and Holland, through the Dutch ports.

The seventh, eighth and ninth centuries – the Dark Ages – saw little progress in wine production. In England the clergy made their wine as a matter of household catering, and for the Mass, while in Europe the Christian missionaries resisted the Barbarian hordes from eastern Europe who sacked villages, churches and vineyards alike. Substantial wine trade with the Netherlands was eventually brought to a halt by the attacks of the Norsemen. However, the Moors, who conquered Spain, improved the culture of the vine there.

Fig. 1

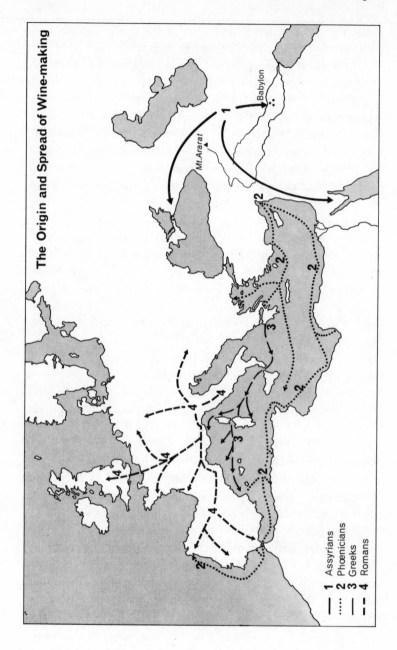

The Origin and Spread of Wine-making

1 Assyrians
2 Phoenicians
3 Greeks
4 Romans

Babylon

Mt. Ararat

In the eleventh century the real period of expansion of the wine industry began. The Normans were now to conquer England, and they knew much about wine. But the growth of wine production and consumption did not stem only from France. The wine industry of Italy, for example, had to support a large and growing demand, and it has been estimated that Florence alone accounted for the consumption of some six million gallons a year at this time. The export of wine became an important part of contemporary trading, and sailings from the Mediterranean to Northern Europe increased as the great fairs in the cities of Northern France and the Netherlands were established.

But it was the influence of kings which was destined to shape the wine-drinking habits of the English. In 1153, Henry Duke of Anjou (later King Henry II of England) married Eleanor of Aquitaine, and she brought him as her dowry the provinces of Gascony and Bordeaux – all the land to the south of the Loire. This was the starting-point of the British wine trade, for the people of Bordeaux wanted English wool, and paid for it in wine to a large extent. As the British could not drink it all, a great wine trade grew up with the Hanseatic states of Germany, and with the Baltic, and though wine accounted for one third of England's imports, much was re-exported.

As the French wines came in, viticulture in England fell into decay. Most of the English vineyards were uprooted to make way for more profitable crops, although monastic vineyards survived until Henry VIII seized the monasteries in the sixteenth century.

The entente with France lasted happily for some hundred and fifty years, but then came famines and plagues (including the Black Death which swept Europe) and wars in which France was our enemy or our opponent in foreign policy. During the French Wars, friendship with Spain naturally encouraged increases in Spanish wine imports. In 1353 England signed the Treaty of Windsor, establishing Portugal as England's oldest ally, and granting her great commercial advantages. England now looked also to Portugal to provide her with wine.

It will be seen that the English market was by no means a monopoly for France. From Germany and the Low Countries came Rhenish wine, and through Genoa came Commandaria from Cyprus, and other sweet Mediterranean wines. In the sixteenth century, sack, a wine similar to present-day sherry, became the favourite wine in England, coming from Jerez and Teneriffe.

The pattern of the English wine trade settled down, with imports mainly from Spain, Italy and Portugal, some from France, and a little from Germany and the Low Countries. However, during the seventeenth century, deterioration in the quality of Italian wines and the imposition of heavy duties on French wines decreased their importance.

As a consequence of the falling-off of French and Italian wine imports, there was an increase in the sale of relatively cheap

Portuguese wine in England, a development encouraged by the
Methuen Treaty of 1703, which revived the spirit of the old
Treaty of Windsor, giving Portuguese wines preferential rates
of duty. As a result, many English wine-merchants made their
headquarters in Oporto and became so important that they set up
their own courts of law there. Many descendants remain there
to this day. Portuguese wine imports rose steadily during the
eighteenth century, until Portuguese wines accounted for two
thirds of all Britain's imports.

The discovery of America and the sea route to India, although
affecting European trade profoundly, did not alter the pattern
of the wine trade in the fifteenth and sixteenth centuries, as the
new territories neither produced nor consumed wine.

The duty on French wine soon became sufficiently prohibitive
to induce alternative drinking habits. Taxes were paid on bulk,
and therefore spirits, because of their greater strength-to-bulk
ratio, attracted less duty. French brandy, under James II, had
become a popular drink by the end of the seventeenth century,
but gin received a boost when William of Orange displaced the
francophile James in 1688, and introduced Hollands gin which,
in its worst form, even the poorest could afford.

Gin could be made cheaply in England – and was. In fact,
the poverty-stricken masses took to the poisonous oblivion of
'gin' as their only release from misery and hardship. Hogarth,
in a famous cartoon depicting 'Gin Lane', showed the drunken
dregs of humanity busy pawning and stealing. The sign over
the gin-shop reads 'Drunk for a penny. Dead drunk 2d. Straw
free'.

So, as the nineteenth century dawned, the social conditions
of England were appalling, as every Dickens-lover will know.
But reform was round the corner. As the new century progressed,
many hitherto unknown elements affected the national scene,
with consequences to the wine and spirit industry. Principally,
the growth of British imperial power brought a greater and more
diversified trade. Imports of South African and Australian wines

appeared for the first time. The policy of Free Trade opened the doors of England to the world's wines and spirits, and this policy was also to be responsible – quite unconsciously – for making Britain the expert in the international wine and spirit industry. Almost every other country supported its domestic wine industry by imposing swingeing duties on imports, and in so doing denied itself this vital knowledge of the wines and spirits of other countries.

After a brief period in the middle of the century, in which Spanish wine formed a major part of Britain's wine imports, French wines again became fashionable, and were imported in quantities comparable with those from Spain and Portugal. Claret was much in demand, and in 1876 seven million gallons of French wines were imported, a record to remain unbroken until 1968.

The lower classes had remained faithful to cheap gin however, and strenuous efforts were made, not only to control its production and sale, but also to wage a war of propaganda against it. In 1860 Gladstone, Chancellor in Lord Palmerston's government, reduced the duties on light wines in an attempt to wean the lower classes off spirits. Eight years later, Gladstone's government was elected on a temperance platform, and introduced much-needed social reforms. But Gladstone failed in his attempt to introduce licensing laws in 1874. Riots ensued in London, which were quelled by troops. Instead, the duty on wines was reduced again, and the basis of duty was changed. A hydrometer, devised by a customs officer named Sikes, was introduced to implement a sliding scale of duties on wines and spirits, according to strength.

The wine-merchants of the day were equal to the situation, and it is said that one toured the streets armed with tracts persuading people to 'sign the Pledge'. With the encouraging exhortation 'You can still drink Port, lad – that's not Ardent Spirits' – the wine-merchant would take an order for port on the spot. Port soon became the Englishman's wine.

The nineteenth century saw the birth of the Salvation Army, which favoured total abstinence, while the Band of Hope campaigned against intoxicants, largely through the enrolment of children. The cause of temperance was however widely pleaded, for the truth was, and is, that wines and spirits in moderation never did anyone any harm and do many a great deal of good. Pasteur in particular wrote and campaigned about the health-giving qualities of wine.

And so to the twentieth century. Port had remained all the fashion since Gladstone's day and with the Portuguese Trade Treaty Acts of 1914 and 1916, the making of port was as strictly controlled by English law as by Portuguese law. By the late 'twenties, however, port started to lose its general popularity and became more associated with post-prandial drinking. Sherry became the more popular wine for social drinking.

Preferential rates of duty given to Empire wines did much to establish a steady trade with South Africa and Australia during the early years of the century.

Another influence which was quick to affect British drinking habits was the Prohibition legislation of the United States of America, which outlawed all alcoholic beverages. Spirits ousted wines on the undercover market for the very logical reason of their lesser bulk and greater 'kick'; spirits, it will be recalled, were carried in the leg of a boot. Many were of amateur origin, tasted horrid and were distinctly harmful. The taste had to be disguised; and that is how the cocktail was born. The cocktail habit remains with us; but today the ingredients are wholesome.

In recent years, drinking habits have been affected more and more by duty changes. Sir Stafford Cripps halved the duty on beverage wines in 1949, bringing them within reach of the ordinary man, and in 1958 Heathcoat Amery reduced the duty on fortified wines also, which gave a boost to this trade. But over the last decade, successive governments have imposed heavier duties than ever before, and this has held back expansion of sales in the better classes of wine.

In spite of this the habit of wine-drinking is spreading, and inexpensive light beverage wine is being consumed in ever-increasing quantities, thanks partly to the 'package tour' which is taking more and more people abroad, where they drink local wines and return with a taste for them. These light wines carry less duty, many of them are very good, and their price is attractive.

The wine trade, then, has followed the explorer and the flag, and in this way the craft has been disseminated throughout the world and through the ages by the Phoenicians, Romans and Greeks; by the French, Spanish and Portuguese; by the Italians, Germans and Dutch; and in lesser degree by the late-developing countries of the other wine-producing areas of the world.

Levels of production

Currently, nearly 7000 million gallons of wine are produced throughout the world each year, and this quantity is increasing. As one gallon of wine fills six standard threequarter-litre bottles, the world output is equivalent to 40,000 million bottles a year, or say a dozen bottles for every man, woman and child on the earth's surface. Much of this wine is very light and unstable and is not exported from the country of origin.

At present, threequarters of the world produce comes from Europe, and the largest individual producers there (in millions of gallons per annum) are France and Italy, about 1400 each; Russia and Spain, about 600 each; Portugal, about 200; and Germany, about 140. Other wine-producing countries in Europe are Yugoslavia, Greece, Switzerland, Hungary, Austria, Bulgaria and Luxembourg.

Wine-producing countries outside Europe but bordering on the Mediterranean include Turkey and the North African countries, especially Algeria, which produces about 200 million gallons per annum.

'Commonwealth' wines come from the Cape area of South Africa, from Australia (mainly from the southeastern regions), and from Cyprus and Malta.

Fig. 3 World wine production, 1971   21

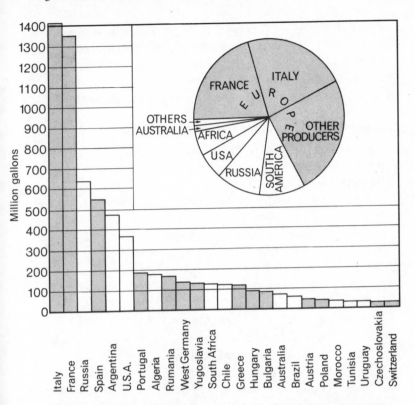

In North America, some wine is produced in Ontario, while 90% of the United States wine is produced in California, the remaining 10% coming from the states of New York and Ohio. The best-known South American producer is Chile, with other wines, hitherto mainly for home consumption, being made in Argentina, Brazil and Paraguay. Argentinian production is about equal to that of Russia and Spain, and is now appearing in foreign markets under brand names, in increasing quantities.

Factors affecting production

A review of the countries producing wine will reveal that only a relatively small area of the world is 'wine-bearing'. Vines will grow practically anywhere outside the polar regions, but their grapes will only provide juice of the quality necessary for conversion into drinkable wine where two climatic conditions prevail. Firstly, there must be enough sun to ripen the grapes. Secondly, the winter must be moderate, yet sufficiently cool to give the vine a chance to rest and restore its strength for the growing and fruiting season.

In England, for example, there is only sufficient sun to ripen a grape crop in the open in two years out of five; and it is not possible to guarantee a frost-free period when the flowers are forming.

In fact the strength of the summer sun does not become sufficient until the latitude of the Rhineland is reached, and even there the crop may easily be upset. So the northern limit of winemaking in the northern hemisphere is controlled by the first condition, the need for enough sun to ripen the grapes. This condition applies equally to the southern limit of wine-making in the southern hemisphere. This 'cold' limit lies roughly at latitudes 50° north and south. On the other hand, the tropics and sub-tropics do not get a cool winter, being warm throughout the year, so that vines planted there would not have the chance to rest before the growing season. This, the second condition, therefore controls the southern limit of the 'wine belt' in the northern hemisphere and the northern limit in the southern hemisphere. The 'hot' limit lies roughly at latitudes 30° north and south.

The map on page 23 shows the limitations of these northern and southern wine belts, and the bar chart on page 21 gives an approximation of the relative shares of world production provided by the countries within them.

Wine-producing areas of the world
As well as being one of the world's two largest producers, France excels in producing wines of the very finest quality and diversity, having many distinct wine regions each producing wines unique in character.

Fig. 4

23

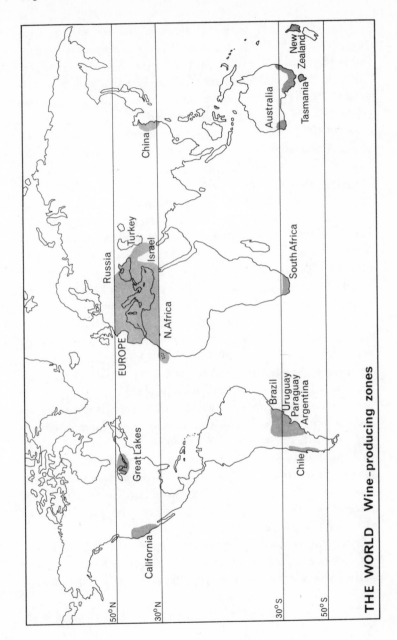

THE WORLD Wine-producing zones

Bordeaux, with its output of some 100 million gallons each year, is subdivided into districts of international reputation – the Médoc, Graves, Sauternes, Entre-deux-Mers, St. Emilion, Côtes de Bourg and Côtes de Blaye. Burgundy, with a smaller production, has several famous districts, such as Chablis, Côte de Nuits, Côte de Beaune and Beaujolais.

Other great regions in France are Champagne, the valleys of the Rhône and Loire, the Midi in the southwest and Alsace near the German border.

From Italy comes a full range of sweet and dry red and white wines, in addition to excellent *apéritif* and dessert wines, and sparkling wines. Unlike the French wines, which are generally known by their area of production, the Italian wines may be labelled according to the grape from which they are made or their place of origin.

The best-known wines of Italy include Vermouth, an aromatic herbal wine; Chianti, a light or full-bodied red wine; Orvieto and Frascati, dry and medium-dry straw-coloured wines; Soave, a dry white wine; Barolo, a big red wine improving with age; Valpolicella, a full-bodied red wine; Asti Spumante, the best-known Italian sparkling wine, white and sweet; and Marsala, a rich, sweet, fortified wine produced in Sicily.

By far the most important wine produced in Spain is sherry, a fortified wine. Nevertheless, a significant part of our supply of inexpensive beverage wines is produced in Spain. Unfortunately, perhaps, many of their wines have in the past been sold under French-type names, as for example 'Spanish Burgundy', and this despite their own particular characteristics which do not pretend to resemble the French products. This practice, however, is no longer permitted.

The better-known Spanish wines include Valdepeñas, Rioja, Tarragona and Malaga. Despite a varied history Spanish wines, particularly sherry, are now enjoying a boom on the British market.

Portugal will forever be associated in the public mind with

Fig. 5

25

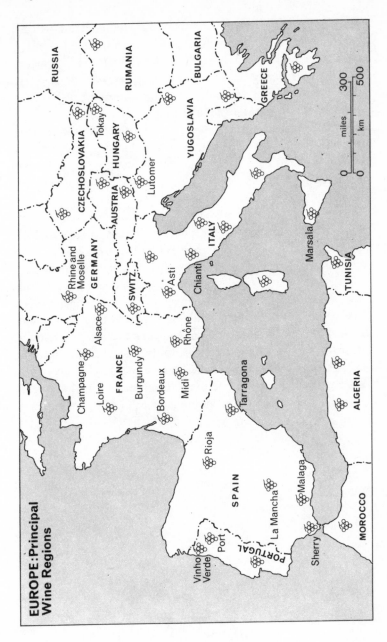

EUROPE: Principal Wine Regions

port, the superb fortified wine from the Douro. But Portugal exports other wines, notably the *vinhos verdes* or 'green wines', made from immature or green grapes. These wines, usually semi-sparkling or *pétillant* in character, are currently very popular in Britain. A range of red, white and rosé wines is also produced throughout the country, much of it for export.

Germany's production is only about two thirds of the volume produced in Portugal, due mainly to the climate at the north of the wine belt. The light German white wines known as Hocks and Moselles from the Rhine and Mosel valleys are renowned throughout the world.

Good wines, though not necessarily great ones, come from South Africa, Australia and Cyprus; they are reliable and of standard quality. Although their 'sherries' may be the best known, a full range of wines is exported from these countries.

There are many other countries, not only in Europe but throughout the wine-producing areas of the world, which export little or no wine; examples are Russia, the United States and South America. It must be remembered that in total only a small fraction of the world's wine output is consumed outside its country of origin, many wines lacking the stability necessary to travel from country to country. However, if such wines are to be found anywhere away from home, it will be in Britain.

The vine and the grower

So numerous are the varieties of wine that the amateur – the lover of wine – is almost prone to lose heart. However, a logical study of those factors which affect the production of wines and determine their characteristics will rapidly show that a sensible working knowledge of wines is not really so difficult to acquire. But in gaining this knowledge the reader should not expect to become an expert: that may take a lifetime.

The importance of natural conditions
In each season of the year the vineyard and the vineyard owner or grower (who in France is called the *vigneron*) respond to nature, and in this respect nature works on two levels. Firstly, because of the Earth's course in the heavens, the seasons, and hence the hours of daylight, and the height and heat of the sun, are predetermined. But nature works also at a secondary level, where such features as the continental land masses and the oceans that separate them set up varying climates, which in turn are affected by other permanent and recurring conditions. Mountains and plains, rivers and valleys, forests and lakes, all contribute to the climate in each country. And although neighbouring regions may share prevalent winds and the same average rainfall, they still have their own very local conditions; spots that will catch the sun or the wind, or where fog or frost will gather. Thus each district has its individual microclimate.

The climate then is a critical factor in wine production. Already, two general bands around the Earth's surface have been identified in which the wine-producing vine may grow, one north and one south of the equator. Between them it is too hot, beyond them too cold. The climate varies within these bands, not only from continent to continent and country to country, but also from district to district. Where the microclimate is suitable for wine production, man-made conditions are superimposed on natural conditions in such a way that the wine product of that district is practically unique and can be identified by the expert.

Traditionally, the growers have made the best use of their microclimate and topography. It will be found that the best vineyards were usually sited away from forest masses, which create excessive humidity, and that the warm aspect was always selected (in Europe this generally means a hill looking to the southeast). The best vineyards have seldom been sited at the top of hills, where exposure to wild weather would damage the crops, or at the bottom of valleys, where cold air and frost may collect. Standing water in a valley may rot the vine or lower the temperature unduly in the cold seasons. (Water can also store heat, however, and help to moderate extremes of temperature.) The average yearly temperature should be 14° to 15°C (57° to 59°F) ideally, and certainly not less than 10°C (50°F), with summer and winter limits of 22°C (72°F) and 3°C (37°F) respectively. To enable the vine to flower, a temperature of 15°C (59°F) or more is necessary.

The grower looks for an average of six to seven hours of sunshine every day from March to September, which may sound reasonable, but he may not always get it. The weather should be cool, even cold for the remainder of the year, so that the sap will withdraw from the canes. In these conditions, the vine will have the rest it needs so that it can flower and bear fruit in the succeeding year. In established vineyard regions, the grower will always have a sufficiently cold winter to rest his vine; the danger is that he will have too much cold.

Fortunately, it is rare for the temperature to drop to −15°C (5°F), at which temperature the vine root splits and dies. The effects of such bad luck can be avoided or mitigated by the grower in choosing hardier, if less productive, strains of vine, and by earthing his vines up for the winter. He may be unlucky

Fig. 6
29

Factors affecting the Taste of Wine	
	*Soil*
	*Climate*
	*Grape*
	*Viticulture*
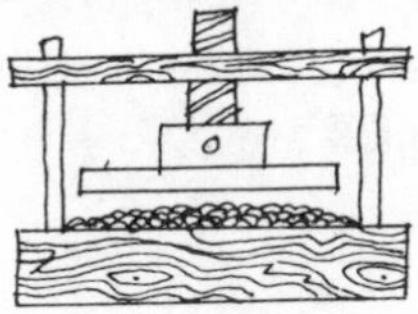	*Vinification*
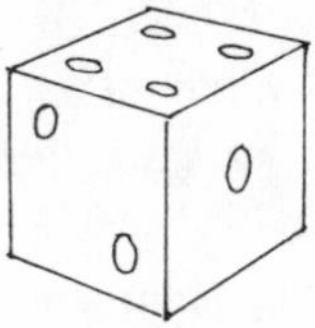	*Luck of the Year*

in a warm winter in not having a frost hard enough to kill the insect and fungus pests, which will then plague him the following year.

The vine needs plenty of sunshine and warmth in summer to ripen the grapes, but too hot a sun will burn the leaves, and only while the leaves are green do they have power to ripen the fruit. On the equatorial sides of the two wine belts, too much heat can produce dull 'flabby' wines, heavy in alcohol, which are useful only for blending. Hail storms in the vineyard are not uncommon in summer, and there is very little that modern science or the grower can do about it. In early summer, hail may rip the young shoots and reduce the yield. Late in the season, hailstones which strike the grapes break the skins, allowing moulds to form and rot them. Grapes so affected turn a dirty brown colour and give an off-flavour, *goût de grêle*, to the wine. Strong winds also have their dangers, particularly during the flowering season, when the pollen that must be taken from flower to flower by insects or by light winds for fertilization, can be blown away in a gale. Unless the flower is fertilized it will not form a grape.

Not surprisingly, the growers and all who gain their living from wine shrug their shoulders or smile as they discuss 'the luck of the year' – rain, hail, frost, wind and sun – each of which contributes to their particular microclimates. Usually it is a shrug *and* a smile, for seldom is their luck wholly good or wholly bad. But there are other factors affecting the ultimate wine produced: the soil in which the vine is planted, the vine itself, and the pests and diseases to which it may fall prey.

Soil

It has been said that 'the best wines come from the poorest soils'. While this cannot be taken literally (for some soils are too poor to grow anything), vineyards seem to flourish where other crops will not, and produce less delicate wines from rich soils. In many fields of agriculture the growth potential of soil is judged by its nitrogen content, which stimulates growth of stem and leaf.

Important to agriculture, nitrogen is less so to horticulture, and the wine-producing vine marks the boundary between the two. It is an agricultural crop requiring horticultural treatment. What the vine needs far more than nitrogen are the mineral elements in the soil, which are essential to the delicate flavours of different wines. In other words, nitrogen will give quantity but minerals will give quality, and the grower will therefore prune each year to confine growth and concentrate the minerals in his crop of fruit.

It is true that the rich grower today has the resources which enable him to adjust nitrogen and mineral content, acidity and drainage, and so do much to compensate for deficiencies in his soil. Therefore it could be argued that the soil is not the all-important factor in wine production that it once was. However such treatments are expensive, and most growers have to take their soil as they find it.

Vineyards are grown on a wide variety of soils. The best sherry vineyards of southern Spain have very chalky soil, with some clay. The vineyards perched on the steep hills of the Douro Valley in northern Portugal, where port is produced, are slaty. In Champagne a poor, thin, loam topsoil covers a chalky base, which drains the vine roots. Bordeaux has poor soils, mostly gravel or pebbles covering a base of limestone, clay and chalk. In Burgundy there is a range from poor granitic acid soil to alkaline limestone. The weathered granite of Alsace is mixed with sandy gravel and alluvial soils, and in the Rhine and Mosel valleys of Germany the soil is mainly slaty, rich in minerals and limestone. The steep stony hills of Tuscany produce Chianti, Italy's best-known wine, and Piedmont, another region for fine Italian wines, has a limestone soil, with a high proportion of iron.

Vineyards are mainly situated in river valleys, where soils tend to be well-drained gravels, sand, alluvial matter, and weathered igneous rocks. Another reason why the old-established vineyards are found by rivers is the transport facility which

the rivers afforded. Before the days of good roads, bulk cargoes
of wine could only be moved by water.

Types of vine and methods of propagation

The soils mentioned are all well-drained and have a low organic
content but quite a high mineral content. Each differs from its
neighbour and, through the grape, produces subtly different
wines. There are also hundreds of grape varieties, each with its
characteristic flavour. Some vines have definite preferences for
certain soils to produce their best wine. As with other plants,
some varieties of vine ripen early and others ripen late. The
grower's choice of vine must rank as the most important decision
in determining the type and quality of his wine, and indeed its
colour; and the grower can choose from hundreds, although
he may well be limited by local wine laws to no more than a dozen,
and for certain wines he is completely ruled both on type and
proportion.

The vine species that grew in the Caucasus in prehistoric
times and spread to stock the vineyards of the world was *vitis
vinifera*, the 'wine-bearing vine'. This species is one of many
hundreds in the botanical family of *Ampelidaceae*, a family which
includes Virginia creeper and many other climbing and creeping
plants. From *vitis vinifera* all the varieties now planted in Europe
have evolved through mutation and cross-breeding, to suit local
soils and climates. The same vine variety, grown in different
regions and processed in different ways, will produce wines of
differing characteristics; again, the same vine variety in different regions can be, and often is, given a different name. Of the
black varieties, some of the famous ones are the Cabernet-
Sauvignon of Bordeaux and the Loire, the Pinot Noir of North
Burgundy and Champagne, the Gamay of the Beaujolais, the
Sangiovese of Chianti in Italy, and the Grenache of Châteauneuf-
du-Pape which, as Garnacha, produces fine Spanish wines.

The white varieties include the Sémillon, which produces
the fine sweet Sauternes, the Sauvignon of Pouilly-sur-Loire,

Opposite: Ancient Egyptian Amphora

the Chardonnay, producing Champagne and fine white Burgundies, the Riesling and Sylvaner of Germany and Alsace, and the Palomino, used in the production of sherry.

Appendix 1 sets out the names of some sixty vine varieties, with cross-references, not only to the districts in which they are used and the types of wine made from them, but also to their local names.

Vines are propagated by rooting cuttings and by grafting, rather like roses. New varieties obtained by crossing are raised from seed in the first instance, for example Riesling × Sylvaner. The young plants are transferred from nurseries to the vineyard at various stages of development. Like all vegetable matter, vines need water, carbon dioxide, light and heat, nutrients and minerals. The roots find the water, some roots delving to low levels, where it is almost permanently available. Other roots, called day roots, take advantage of water from the least shower. In humid conditions, the vine can also absorb water through its leaves.

The most important constituent of the grape to the making of wine is sugar. How does it get there? Sugar is a carbohydrate, as every slimmer knows, and is a complex molecule; grape sugar comprises a total of 24 carbon, hydrogen, and oxygen atoms – $C_6H_{12}O_6$. The leaves of the vine are the factories. When sunlight falls on their green matter, chlorophyll, carbon dioxide (CO_2) is drawn from the air to combine with water (H_2O) drawn from the soil via the roots and the vine stem, and they are bound together to make sugar. Some oxygen is left over, and is released to the air. The circulating sap takes the sugar and stores it in the growing grapes. The grower will take care to cut back long-growing shoots in summer, as they would consume some of the sugar for their own growth.

All growing and decomposing organic matter produces carbon dioxide, and its concentration in the air is greatest at the end of the night. The process of assimilation – of turning this into sugar – is therefore most effective on southeasterly slopes,

Opposite: Clos-de-Vougeot and its Château in Burgundy

which receive the energy of the early morning sun. Also, at this time haze and dust are least, so that the sun's rays are not obscured. Moreover, in the higher latitudes nearer to the poles, it is not only the winter cold that limits grape production, but also the greater absorption of the sun's energy in having to penetrate the atmosphere at a more oblique angle.

Pruning of the vine takes place during the winter. This time of year is chosen because the sap has withdrawn from the canes, and the vine will not therefore 'bleed' when cut. As with roses, nearly all the previous year's growth is cut away, leaving a selected few buds to provide the new year's growth. It is important to prune the vine hard, for each cane may grow as much as fifteen feet every year. The time of pruning also is important: the later it is pruned, the later it will flower. However, while there is more danger of bleeding with late pruning, which will weaken the vine, there is less danger of a late frost killing the flowers.

But the question arises: when is the grower pruning, and when is he training the vine? For the answer it is necessary to look at the objectives. Fundamentally, pruning is the cutting out of unwanted growth with the object of conserving quality in a reduced quantity of produce; pruning ensures that the vine will use the sun's energy to store sugar in a controlled crop of grapes which have taken the optimal goodness from the soil, rather than squandering that energy in luxuriant foliage and long shoots. Training, on the other hand, is the cultivation of an eventual plant shape which is conducive to production of the best fruit. Therefore, when the grower prunes he will be selective, taking away only those parts of the vine which are not essential to the eventual vine shape. It must be remembered that the essential shape of the vine is dictated not by the grower, but by the natural condition of the vineyard – latitude, height, part of slope and microclimate.

So as the vines grow, the grower sets about training them from year to year. If there is danger of too much frost, the vines will

Fig. 7   35

Styles of Vine Training

Guyot Simple   Guyot Double   Gobelet   Bush

Low Styles

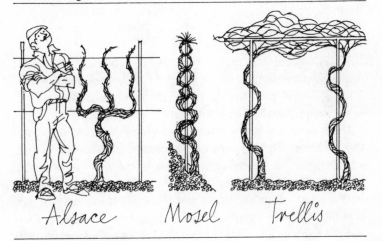

Alsace   Mosel   Trellis

High Styles

be trained higher from the ground. Or, if it is desired to get
maximum heat from the soil, the vines will be trained near to
the ground. Incidentally, too much heat can also be a disadvan-
tage, and in very hot regions it may be necessary to grow the
vines on trellises high above the ground. Fig. 7 shows the
methods of training the vine adopted in a number of regions.

In the Guyot Double system, much used in northern Europe,
two shoots are first trained, from which the fruit-bearing shoots
develop over a period of four years. Generally, the planting
distances are four feet between vines in one row and five feet
between rows. However, the Lenz Moser system, introduced
as an economy, provides nine or ten feet between rows to admit
tractors for cultivation, spraying and harvesting purposes.
Typical of the bush system is the Gobelet, used in the Beaujolais,
where the shoots are tied together at the top, simulating the
shape of a goblet. The Alsace and Mosel methods show the tall
vines best shaped for the steep slopes. In parts of southern
Europe, where the sun is very hot, the trellis method is ideal;
here the grapes are suspended high over the surface, where
they suffer less from overheating by reflection of the sun's rays
from the ground.

Pests and diseases

Like all agricultural crops, the vine is subject to pests and
diseases, in the form of birds, insects, fungi, viruses and weeds.
The *vigneron* has steadily mastered the catastrophes of the
last century, but the battle with nature is a constant one.

Birds can cause severe damage, and there is no real answer to
the problem. Children beating saucepans with spoons help to
scatter them, but deterrents such as scarecrows are soon treated
with the familiarity they deserve. Sprays are unsatisfactory
because they affect the grape and the vine. It can only be said
that birds present a problem which the grower is happy to share
with neighbouring fruit farmers. One can understand why
roasted ortolans and thrush pâté are available in vineyard areas.

Because the English were keen botanists, and inveterate travellers, plants from all over the world came to Kew Gardens. Unfortunately, some brought pests and diseases with them. One of the earlier fungi to reach Europe was *Oïdium Tuckeri*, a 'powdery mildew' which covered the grapes, splitting and rotting them. Hardly had this been conquered, when the dreaded *Phylloxera Vastatrix* arrived accidentally on the American species *vitis riparia*, imported to various European countries from the eastern states of North America between 1858 and 1862. By the end of the century most European vineyards had had to be uprooted because of this louse-like, almost invisible, aphid, producing an acute shortage of wine. In this situation, blended and poor quality wines were marketed.

Since *vitis riparia* and the other American varieties *rupestris* and *berlandieri* did not seem to suffer from the pest, and bore grapes, some growers planted them and made wine from them. The wines had an unmistakable, pungent flavour, repugnant to those who liked the fine wines of earlier years; nevertheless people drank them, and hoarded their remaining stocks of pre-*Phylloxera* wine for great occasions. Some, however, acquired a taste for the 'fox wine' as it was called, and grew even to prefer it. A few peasant farmers still make wine from these vines for their own use, and the trouble is that such grapes can unknowingly be bought in by the wine cooperatives. A small quantity of fox grapes will give a distinct off-flavour to a whole vat of wine, much as wild garlic, eaten by one cow, can taint a whole county's milk. So these varieties, and hybrids bred from them, are banned in nearly every region, and severe penalties imposed on those who grow them.

The cure, if cure be the eradication of the pest in one vineyard, was to uproot and burn the vines, and to sterilize the soil. But that hardly touched the cause, and certainly did nothing to meet the effect – no vineyard, no wine. Scientists provided the answer. The *riparia* vine species, which had brought the pest to Europe, was found to be resistant to it, whereas the European *vinifera* species was not. As *Phylloxera* caused its worst damage to the roots, grafting was found to be the answer. European 'scions' could be grafted on to resistant American root-stocks, and this practice has become standard throughout the world, wherever *vitis vinifera* is grown. The *Phylloxera* is so hardy that there is no absolute remedy, and the dangers that it represents will always be with the grower. Before replanting a vineyard, therefore, the soil is always dressed with strong insecticides.

A summary of these afflictions and a number of others is given in Appendix 2, page 172.

The partial defence against *Phylloxera*, the grafting of European *vinifera* scions on to American *riparia* stocks, presented little problem to the French. Their nurserymen were already experts in the art of grafting, and soon perfected techniques to meet an enormous demand for grafts to restock the lost vineyards of Europe.

A straightforward graft may be made by taking a scion of the desired, non-resistant variety and a root-stock of the resistant American variety, each of the same diameter, cutting each through on the diagonal, and binding the upper section of the scion to the lower section of the stock. More safely, an open V is cut in the stock, and the scion cut into a pointed section to fit into it.

The French use a 'whip and tongue' graft, which combines these two principles, giving a maximum surface area of 'cambium' in contact. Fig. 8 shows the principle of these grafts. The French call the whip and tongue graft *la greffe anglaise*, which suggests that it may have been of English origin. The *maître greffeur*, whose uncanny skill enables him to cut and fit a graft by eye with the precision of a cabinet-maker, has outlived the grafting machine which promptly appeared on the market after the great *Phylloxera* plague.

In bench grafting, the method used in colder climates, the grafts are packed in boxes, covered with charcoal and soil, and left to grow together in greenhouses. After about three months,

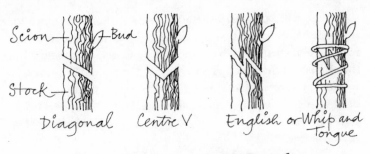

Fig. 8   *Main types of Graft*

those which have taken are planted out in nurseries to grow and harden off during the summer and following winter. Thence they go for final planting in the vineyards in the following spring. In warmer climates, where bedding-out is an unnecessary expense, the root-stocks are planted straight into their final position in the vineyards. When spring comes, their shoots and leaves are removed, and scions from *vitis vinifera* are grafted straight on to the bare stocks.

The successful vineyard proprietor with a technical training and long experience of the climate, the soil, the vine, the methods of pruning and training, the pests and diseases, and the hazards of nature, is equipped to take them all in his stride, and his yearly cycle of vineyard management will start after the vintage has been finished, in October or early November each year. First he will tidy up, and providing the soil is dry, the winter plough-ing will begin and continue into December. He will plough the soil up to the roots of the vines for winter protection and the roots may also be mulched with compost for the same purpose. From December to February the vine needs light frost to kill disease and also to help it to rest. From January onwards the vineyard will be pruned, and the aim is always quality, not quantity. Pruning is not only a very skilled task but it is also compelled by law in France and many other countries. In the spring, as soon as the vine shoots start to grow, they will be attached to stakes and wires in many districts. If manure is spread, it will be ploughed under, and, at the same time, the soil that has been ploughed up to the roots in November will now be ploughed away from them. Young grafts brought from the nursery in their second year will be planted out. Rain is now wanted to make a good spring growth. Late frosts are a real danger and, to combat these, fires are lit in the vineyards to create air circulation, for frosts at this time of year only form when the air is still.

In late May or early June the vine will flower, and the grower's annual battle with pest and disease will begin. Indeed if meteorological conditions have been bad he may already have started spraying against mildew during April. When the flowers are on the vine, mild weather is wanted, for too much wind will scatter the flowers and the pollen will be lost. To encourage pollination, the grower may have planted roses at the end of the rows in the vineyard; the vine flower is insignificant to look at, and the roses will attract the bees and set them about their task.

Not only does the grower need clement weather during flowering, but the weather in the hundred days which follow before the grapes are ripe is critical. Some rain at first, to swell the grapes, is needed, followed by hot sunshine to ripen them. But if all goes well, at the end of September or early in October, the grapes will be fully ripe and they can be picked. This is hard work demanding a great deal of labour for about three to four weeks. People come from all over the country, and even from abroad, to help with the vintage.

Usually the pickers in the vineyard use wooden baskets, cutting the grape bunches carefully from the vine with knives or secateurs. Their baskets are emptied into bigger baskets or hods, carried on the backs of stronger members of the team. The loaded weight at this stage is about one hundredweight (50 kg), and the hod is then carried to the road for transfer to large tractor-drawn tubs or modern tipper lorries. And so the grapes make their way to the winery, handled tenderly and carefully at every stage in order to be perfect for vinification.

The making of wine

As the hot hundred days draw to their end, the ripened grapes are harvested and brought to the winery in baskets or other containers in much the same way as they have been for a thousand years or more. In a matter of minutes, their transformation into wine will begin. But the process will bear very careful study, for the chemical action of fermentation – the conversion of sugar into alcohol – is fundamental to all alcoholic drinks; not only to still, sparkling and fortified wines, but also to spirits, liqueurs and beers, even though some variations and further processes will be applied for individual beverages.

The grape

First, a study of the grape itself will explain much that is to follow. If a grape, say a black grape, is put into the mouth and the teeth burst the skin, instantly a fruity sweetness is noticeable, quite different from the flat sweetness of a lump of cane sugar. From this, and from the moisture, the presence of sugar and water in the grape is instantly established. But also a taste quite different from the taste of wine is apparent; this comes from the fruit acids and their compounds within the grape. If the grape skin is next crushed between the teeth, a sensation of bitterness follows, coming from the tannin in the skin; and if a small part of the grape stalk were also bitten, the same bitter taste of tannin would be apparent. However, if one of the pips is crushed by the teeth a different and altogether unpleasant bitterness would be tasted, a bitterness quite unacceptable in wine.

Next, observation of the grape yields more essential information. If a black and a white grape are sliced through the centre, and the cross-sections of each are compared, it will be seen that the jelly-like substance in the middle, composed of juice and

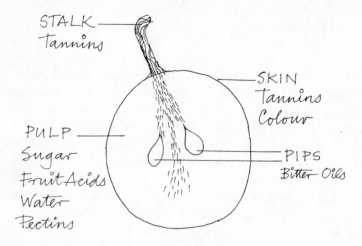

STALK
Tannins

SKIN
Tannins
Colour

PULP
Sugar
Fruit Acids
Water
Pectins

PIPS
Bitter Oils

Fig. 9   *The Grape*

pectins, is a pale green or yellow in colour. So the colour of red wines cannot come from the centre, it must come from the skin of the black grape. Red wine can only be made from black grapes, but white wines can in fact be made from white or black grapes, provided that, in the latter case, the grape skins are removed before fermentation begins.

On the outside of grapes is a whitish bloom, more easily seen on a black grape, although still quite apparent on a white grape. This waxy substance has trapped a mass of organisms, of which three main kinds are important to the wine-maker. Firstly, there are wild yeasts, of which there are some ten million per grape. Secondly, there are about 100,000 wine yeasts, or one for every 100 wild yeasts. The wine yeast *saccharomyces ellipsoideus* ('the potato-shaped fungus that lives on sugar'), is in fact first cousin to the truffle and second cousin to the mushroom. And thirdly, there are bacteria, principally acetobacter, of which there are also about 100,000. The yeasts and bacteria are carried on to the grape by insects, mostly fruit flies, and also float in the air and stick on the grapes. These are all microscopic single-celled living organisms, containing enzymes which will work on the constituents of the grape. Of great importance to the wine-maker is the fact that the wild yeasts and the acetobacter are 'aerobic', that is to say, they can only work in the presence of oxygen. Only the wine yeasts are anaerobic (able to work in the absence of oxygen), so the unwanted wild yeasts and acetobacter can be put out of action by excluding air from the process.

Yeasts feed on sugar, changing it to alcohol by means of their enzymes, on contact. As the enzymes do their work, performing much the same role as machine tools in a factory, gas is given off, so that the whole mixture bubbles and ferments. The wild yeasts, sometimes called 'apiculate' because of their lemon shape, start to work immediately and ferment violently until 4% of alcohol has been produced, at which concentration they will die. The wine yeasts, although slow starters, will then go on producing alcohol up to 16% to 18%. Acetobacter is a real danger, for all that it does is to work on the alcohol and produce vinegar, so it must be prevented as effectively as possible at the earliest opportunity.

Vinification

The atmosphere of a European winery, whether it be a château on the Gironde, a schloss on the Rhine, or a monastery on the Danube, is essentially ageless; stone predominates, and its worn surfaces bear evidence of the workings of machines, some of them primitive, which have served the wine-maker through the ages. It is here that the vintage is received into the first year *chai*. This low building houses the crusher-destalker, which separates the stalks and breaks the skins of the grapes, putting the yeast into contact with the sugar. This equipment has almost entirely displaced the old *lagar*, the shallow trough in which men trod the grapes, either with bare feet or with special boots, enabling the grape skins to be broken without the pips being crushed. Under *lagar* conditions, the wild yeasts started the natural fermentation process and died at 4% of alcohol concentration. The wine yeasts took over the fermentation and continued until either an alcohol concentration of 16% to 18% killed them or no sugar was left to convert. Meanwhile, the *lagar* being open to the air, the acetobacter would convert the alcohol to vinegar, and, if the *lagar* were abandoned, other bacteria would eventually turn the vinegar to water, completing the natural cycle.

Replacing the original *lagar*, a crushing machine and a destalking apparatus were devised. Then came a crusher-destalker, combining both operations, from which the grape pulp was pumped into open wooden vats holding hundreds of gallons. Modern vats, which can be sealed, are made of stainless steel, or of cement lined with tiles or glass. The grape stalks which, together with the spent grape skins recovered later, are known in France as *marc*, are boiled down to produce a spirit of varying quality called *eau-de-vie-de-marc*, or colloquially *marc*.

The grapes and their skins are now known as 'must', and in the vats the yeast will work on the sugar in the process of controlled fermentation. The first step, even before fermentation can begin, may be to add sulphur dioxide. This is called 'sulphuring' and it has two effects. Firstly, the sulphur dioxide, being hungry for oxygen, will take up oxygen from the must, and secondly it will form a coating over the top, preventing the air from getting to the must. This coating stops the wild yeasts and the acetobacter from working, because they are aerobic. The anaerobic wine yeasts are left to carry on the fermentation alone. The principles of natural and controlled fermentation are demonstrated in Fig. 10, page 46.

The sugar, produced in the fruit by assimilation, is ready for its transformation by yeast into alcohol, ethyl alcohol (not to be confused with the poisonous methyl alcohol contained in methylated spirits) and carbon dioxide. Mostly the sugar found in grapes is glucose, but there are many other types of sugar. As individual enzymes will only work on particular sugars, it is perhaps fortunate that the yeasts peculiar to one vineyard usually contain the best enzymes for its wine.

Those who understand a little chemistry can see from Fig. 10 that the glucose molecule is composed of six atoms of carbon, twelve of hydrogen and six of oxygen. It is, in fact, a carbohydrate. All that the yeast with its enzymes is doing is to rearrange this molecule in a different way, to produce two other molecules. This classic equation sets out correctly the molecular change from glucose to alcohol and carbon dioxide, but it conceals behind its simplicity a complex chain of processes by which the conversion actually comes about.

While it is sufficient here to remember that grape sugar influenced by yeast enzymes is turned into ethyl alcohol and carbon dioxide, one fact of the greatest importance must not be overlooked. In the complex reaction that produces this result, fractional quantities of sugar and intermediate compounds get lost on the way and react with other substances like the fruit acids and tannins in the must. These compounds fail to become alcohol and are turned instead into other organic compounds, aldehydes, ketones and esters, which give flavour to the wine. For this the world should be truly grateful, for a plain, simple mixture of ethyl alcohol and water would have no taste at all.

In order to control the production of his wine, the winemaker needs to know certain facts about the must. It is vital that he knows the sugar content, for this will tell him how much alcohol the must is capable of making. There are laws in most countries which specify the minimum alcoholic strength of wines; alcohol is a powerful preservative and will ensure that the wine will remain at its best. A hydrometer is used to measure the specific gravity of the must, which indicates the sugar content accurately, and hence the alcohol potential. The law may allow the wine-maker to add limited quantities of sugar, should the must show insufficient alcohol potential. This process of enrichment, or improvement, is generally called chaptalization,

Fig. 10

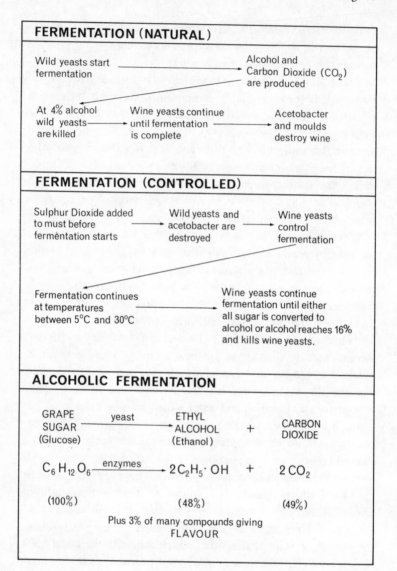

FERMENTATION (NATURAL)

Wild yeasts start fermentation ──────────→ Alcohol and Carbon Dioxide (CO_2) are produced

At 4% alcohol wild yeasts are killed ──→ Wine yeasts continue until fermentation is complete ──→ Acetobacter and moulds destroy wine

FERMENTATION (CONTROLLED)

Sulphur Dioxide added to must before fermentation starts ──→ Wild yeasts and acetobacter are destroyed ──→ Wine yeasts control fermentation

Fermentation continues at temperatures between 5°C and 30°C ──→ Wine yeasts continue fermentation until either all sugar is converted to alcohol or alcohol reaches 16% and kills wine yeasts.

ALCOHOLIC FERMENTATION

GRAPE SUGAR (Glucose) ──yeast──→ ETHYL ALCOHOL (Ethanol) + CARBON DIOXIDE

$$C_6H_{12}O_6 \xrightarrow{enzymes} 2C_2H_5 \cdot OH + 2CO_2$$

(100%) (48%) (49%)

Plus 3% of many compounds giving
FLAVOUR

after the French scientist Chaptal who first devised the method. It is important to remember that additional sugar may only be used to increase the alcohol potential of the wine, and not to increase its sweetness. The must is sucked up from the vat below and put through a mixing machine where ordinary cane sugar is added. If too much is added the flavour of the wine will be spoiled, hence the strict legal control.

The wine-maker needs also to know the acidity of his must, because the fruit acids in the grape affect the working of the yeast. The wine-maker may, as allowed by local laws, control the acidity by adding water or acidifying agents such as gypsum.

As the fermentation gets under way there is need for strict control, and a vat control chart logs the progress of the fermentation. Each day the specific gravity is plotted, showing the wine-maker the progress made by the yeast in converting the sugar to alcohol. As the alcohol increases, the sugar decreases and the specific gravity will drop.

Another line is plotted on the chart, and this relates to the temperature. Temperature control is very important indeed, because fermentation generates heat, and the *saccharomyces* yeasts are very sensitive to heat and cold. They cannot operate below 5°C (40°F), nor above 30°C (90°F). Nor is this the only difficulty, for if must, while fermenting, goes outside this temperature range, fermentation will stop. This is known as 'sticking'. It may not be possible to restart fermentation, particularly if it has been too hot, as changes may have taken place in the sugars to spoil the wine. To avoid this danger the must has to be cooled in hot countries and may have to be gently warmed in cold countries.

Within the safe temperature range, heat will accelerate fermentation, and the quicker the must ferments within this range, the less risk there is of acetobacter breaking down the alcohol. There are various ways in which the wine-maker may keep the temperature within safe limits. Sometimes the wine must be pumped through heated radiators to keep it at a sufficiently high temperature, but more usually it must be cooled. The simplest way is to pump must drawn from the bottom of the vat up to the top, cooling it as it passes through the pipe outside the vat. If a drastic reduction in temperature is necessary, the wine may be pumped through cooling radiators, before being pumped to the top of the vat. This process has another advantage. In making red wine, grape skins are included in the must, and form a floating 'cap' in the vat; and in red wine production the colour must be drawn out of the skins. This can only be done by constant contact with the alcohol in the must, and the pumping of the must over the skins ensures this continual dissolving of colour by the alcohol.

There are other methods of cooling the must. Where modern vats of stainless steel are used, a constant film of cold water may be run over the sides, and in other cases water is sprayed on to hessian wrapped round vats in the open, cooling them as the water evaporates in the sun and breeze.

'Bubble caps', valves which enable the carbon dioxide to escape without admitting any air or bacteria, may be fitted on the tops of vats. The caps can be adjusted to give fermentation under regulated pressure. This method is often referred to as *macération carbonique*.

After a day or so, the first violent fermentation dies down. The wine will go on fermenting for a further period of up to four weeks, depending on the kind of wine being made. For red wine the must contains the skins, which will continue to be fermented in the vat until the required amount of colour and tannin has been drawn from them. At this point, the vat will contain a mixture of liquid (for most of the juice will have been drawn out of the grapes) and skins. The liquid, 'running wine' or *vin de goutte* as it is called in France, will be run off from the bottom of the vat, into casks or another vat, leaving the vat partly filled with *marc*.

There will however, be a large quantity of liquid left in this

Opposite: Top left – Soil: Châteauneuf-du-Pape, Rhône region; Top right – Soil: Port Region of the Douro valley; Bottom left – Soil: Champagne Region; Bottom right – Soil: Bordeaux Region

mass, which will not be wasted. In old types of vat, the mass had to be shovelled out of the top of the vat for further pressing, but modern designs include hatches at the bottom, which facilitate removal of the *marc*.

Today, the *marc* is moved into a press, where the remaining juice is recovered. Naturally, this juice – the *vin de presse* – is much stronger in tannin than the *vin de goutte*. The wine-maker must decide whether he will add all, some or none of this press wine to his *vin de goutte*.

The first presses were of vertical design, worked by a screw or hydraulic pressure. Slightly more gentle than the hydraulic press is the screw press shown in Fig. 11. The mechanism of this screw press rotates, drawing two end-plates together so that the *marc* between them is crushed. As the mechanism is reversed, chains break up the squashed mass of grape skins, so that they are ready to be pressed several more times.

Delicate wines require an even gentler pressing process, which can be provided by another type of cylindrical press which

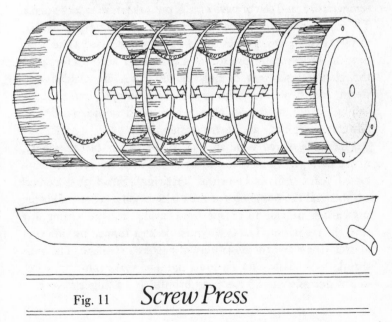

Fig. 11   *Screw Press*

Opposite: Top – Vines trained high; Bottom – Vines trained low

contains an inflatable rubber bag. The press is filled with *marc* and rotated, when the large rubber bag is inflated, and gently and firmly presses the grape skins against the side. The pressure is then released, rotation being continued to allow the grape skins to break up again. Then the process is repeated, as often as required.

In the large cooperatives the volume of production does not allow such individual treatment, and batteries of continuous presses are used, working on the principle of a mincing machine, with the mass being pressed forward against the resistance of its own weight, or of a screw-restricted orifice.

The skins and pips coming from all these presses will eventually be quite dry, but still contain a little sugar. After wetting, they will be fermented again, and then distilled to produce *eau-de-vie-de-marc* in France, or *grappa* in Italy or *bagaçeira* in Portugal; so nothing at all is wasted.

Although the first fermentation is over, the process will continue for up to a month, or even longer, depending upon the temperature, and so the new wine is put to mature in large casks. The casks are mostly made of wood, and vary somewhat in size; in the Gironde small casks called *barriques* are used. The casks have to be carefully purged of the lurking acetobacter, even though the casks may be new. So first they are scalded with steam, and then either sulphur dioxide is pumped into them, or sulphur candles – pieces of paper or cloth impregnated with flowers of sulphur – are burned inside them.

The casks of red wine are put in the cellars of the winery, where they will mature, according to the wine variety, from two to ten years. This is known as 'cellaring'. Small glass conical weights seal the bungholes of the casks in some cellars, allowing any carbon dioxide to escape from inside, but preventing any air from getting in. The casks must be kept topped up, in order to exclude air and the possibility of bacterial spoilage. The wine shrinks as it cools, and a certain amount soaks into the wood, so it is necessary to fill the casks brimful at least once a week.

During the first three months of maturation the wine will throw a sediment, consisting of dead yeasts which have either starved, having consumed all the sugar, or expired from a surfeit of alcohol. The wine must be removed from the dead yeasts because these will decompose quite quickly, and give an off-flavour to the wine. The wine is therefore carefully pumped from one cask to another, leaving the lees at the bottom of the first. Air is pumped into the first cask, forcing the wine into the new one, by 'pushing'. To suck it up might disturb the lees at the bottom, frustrating the whole operation. This process is called 'racking'.

As the last of the wine is transferred to the new cask, it is examined with great care for the first signs of any sediment; and at that moment the racking stops. The lees are not wasted; they go for distillation into *eau-de-vie-de-marc*.

The operation of racking is done for red wine once every three months, as the alcohols and tannins combine to form a much heavier deposit than in white wines. Tannin is very important, however, in clearing wine, as it gathers a lot of the jelly-like protein substances which would otherwise make a wine cloudy. But tannin will not clear all such substances, and more help is necessary, so wines are 'fined' before they are bottled. Fining may be done with a gelatinous substance such as isinglass or white of egg. In Bordeaux, egg whites – usually about six per forty-eight gallon *barrique* – are mixed with a little wine in a bowl, using a small heather whisk. This mixture is then thoroughly stirred into the wine in the cask. The tannin and egg whites combine to form a gummy substance which drags all the protein matter down to the bottom of the cask, leaving the wine above clear and crystal bright. After settling for three weeks the wine is again racked.

Another method is to mix the wine thoroughly with an absorbent earth, such as kieselguhr, which will absorb the protein haze, and then to filter this through very fine filters.

The period of cellaring serves two purposes. It allows the wine to clear, or 'fall bright' in wine-makers' language, and to mature.

The making of white wine differs from the making of red wine, in that the skins are not required. For this reason, grapes for white wine, which may be either black or white, because the juice of both is white, are not crushed and vatted with their skins, as in the production of red wine. Instead they go straight to the press, before they have a chance to start fermenting, and the juice pressed out of them is immediately separated to ferment. Enough of the yeasts will have been washed off the skins to make fermentation possible, and the dry skins are put to distillation. Because they lack the tannin from the skins, white wines do not take quite so long to mature as red wines – usually six months to a year.

Rosé wines can be made in several ways. The classic method is to start the process as for red wine, but to remove the juice from the skins after only a short while. This period could vary from twenty-four to forty-eight hours, depending on the amount of colour required in the wine, and the temperature. A second and very simple method of producing rosé wine is by mixing a very little red wine with a large quantity of white wine. Or again, a small quantity of black grapes may be fermented on the skins with a large quantity of white grapes. It should however be noted that white wine made by fermenting white grapes on their skins may tend to be harsh from the resulting high tannin content. The maturation of rosé wines may last a little longer than for white wines.

Maturation periods will vary quite considerably for different wines; and furthermore, beverage wines will continue to mature in storage, whether in tank, vat or bottle. Wine is a mixture of many things, which continue to act on each other until the wine is finally consumed. There is the alcohol, there are the fruit acids, and there are other substances, such as pectins and tannin, which existed in the original grape. The long interaction during maturation produces a gradual and constant change, so that a young wine does not taste or look the same as an old wine.

Beverage wines

Reviewed in the light of certain facts, it is not surprising that the wines of France are held up to the whole world as examples of character and quality. The latitude of France is ideal for wine production, and most of her 200,000 square miles is fertile agricultural land. For these reasons the grape crops are heavy. Wine production in France has become a major industry to an extent which no other country of Europe can match. The continuous production of wine in volume and variety from the mediaeval period or earlier has given France a knowledge which is yet unequalled. The vines have been selected and bred to complement the soils; the craft of the vineyard has been perfected; the taste for wine of differing characteristics has been measured; the methods of making wine have been adapted to present-day requirements and have made full use of modern scientific developments; and the benefits of research are in the bottle.

The *Appellation Contrôlée* system set up under French law classifies all major vineyards, and such vineyards have been given a right to use certain place-names as an indication of origin. They must be within the official area of *Appellation* and obey many constraints concerning the density of vines, the types of vines planted, the production per acre, and alcoholic strength. This ensures that a Beaujolais *Appellation Contrôlée* is a genuine wine from the legally limited Beaujolais area. French law is sufficiently hard on the transgressor for the purchaser to believe in the label.

The wines of Bordeaux
The areas of France where some of the finest still wines are produced centre on the regions of Bordeaux and Burgundy. The

Fig. 12

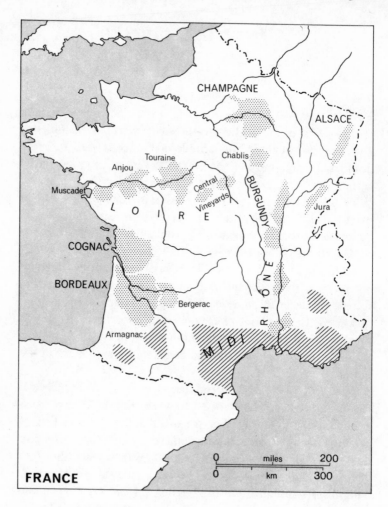

FRANCE

red wines, or clarets, of Bordeaux have been described as the best-known and most popular beverage wines in the world. There are both red and white Bordeaux wines, but the production of claret is somewhat in excess of that of white wine. The Bordeaux region has two rivers, the Garonne and the Dordogne, which meet about ten miles north of the city of Bordeaux; their estuary then takes the name Gironde, as the river broadens out and flows on some forty miles to the sea. This river, the Gironde, gives its name to the *Département* in which all Bordeaux wines are produced.

The valleys of these rivers and the land lying between them are covered with vineyards. The region is divided into six principal districts; in each district there are many small villages known as *communes*, and within these *communes* lie individual châteaux, or vineyards. By these distinctions, the qualities of all Bordeaux wines are indicated on their labels. The mere description 'Red Bordeaux' or 'White Bordeaux' denotes the cheapest of them, but those bearing the name of a district will be of better quality, and individual characteristics will start to be noticeable. If the label also states the village of origin, the wine should again be of better quality, while those bearing the names of the great châteaux vineyards will be the best.

There are great châteaux, and humble: a classification founded on quality, not quantity, for some of the finest châteaux produce little wine. Classifications based on popularity, as measured by price, have been made for a long time; the most famous was the classification of the 1855 Paris *Exposition* which classified the wines of the Gironde into five categories of Great Growths (*Grands Crus Classés*), followed by the categories Exceptional Growths and Bourgeois and Artisan Growths. This ordering of estates is today questioned, but is still generally acceptable as a guide. The 1855 classification is a valuable aid to the understanding of Bordeaux and Burgundy labels, and is reproduced in Appendix 3, page 176.

The area to the northwest of the city of Bordeaux is the Médoc, where the finest claret is produced. South of Bordeaux, to the west of the Garonne, lies the Graves district, taking its name from the gravelly soil; this district is famous for both red and white wines, which are of excellent quality, but which lack the panache of the equivalent wines of the Médoc. Though the wines of Graves are often looked upon as being white and dry, Graves also produces good quality red wines and some sweet and semi-sweet white wines. Château Haut-Brion is the most famous red Graves, an 1855 'first-class growth'.

Enclosed by the Graves district, 30 miles southeast of Bordeaux, the Sauternes district lies on the left bank of the Garonne. Here the world-renowned sweet white wines of Sauternes and Barsac are produced, from grapes which have been affected by *botrytis cinerea* in ideal weather. This produces the condition known as *pourriture noble* ('noble rot'), in which the grapes shrivel to a raisin-like state and their sugar becomes very concentrated.

Across the Garonne from Graves is the district known as Entre-deux-Mers, 'between two rivers', the triangular area formed by the confluence of the Garonne and the Dordogne and the *Département* boundary. Here less distinguished wines, predominantly white, are made, which nevertheless are entitled to their own particular quality wine designation. Two famous districts lie to the north of the River Dordogne; the area surrounding St. Emilion, and Pomerol, where exquisite clarets challenging those from the Médoc are made.

Only the principal districts of Bordeaux have so far been mentioned. But there are minor districts of the region whose finest wines are just as good as the lesser wines of the better-known districts: Côtes de Blaye, Côtes de Bourg, Côtes de Fronsac, Premières Côtes de Bordeaux and Loupiac.

Most clarets are dry or medium-dry and of lighter texture and body than the red Burgundies and Rhône wines. This is due largely to the proximity of the Bay of Biscay, which tends to temper the climate. Even the clarets of St. Emilion, produced some fifty miles inland, are slightly heavier.

Fig. 13   57

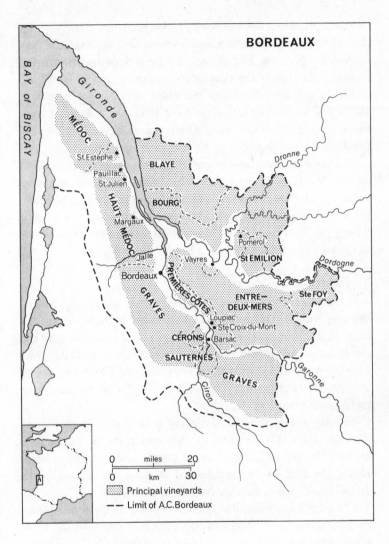

BORDEAUX

BAY of BISCAY

Gironde

MÉDOC

St.Estephe
Pauillac
St.Julien

BLAYE

BOURG

HAUT-MÉDOC

Margaux

Dronne

Jalle

Vayres

Pomerol

St EMILION

Dordogne

Bordeaux

PREMIÈRES CÔTES

GRAVES

ENTRE—
DEUX-MERS

Ste FOY

Loupiac
Ste Croix-du-Mont

CÉRONS   Barsac

SAUTERNES

GRAVES

Ciron

Garonne

0   miles   20
0   km   30

▒ Principal vineyards
— — Limit of A.C. Bordeaux

Bordeaux wines when young can be hard and astringent, although they will age into wines far more delicate than the full-bodied Burgundies. The analogy has been drawn with man and woman – Burgundy the heavier and stronger, soft in youth and duller in old age; Bordeaux the more delicate, yet harder in youth and mellowing into a far more attractive old age. Moodiness, seen in Bordeaux wines which can occasionally fall out of condition, is perhaps also in the feminine character.

The range and quality of Bordeaux wines should not be under-estimated. They range from light golden to deep purple in colour, and between them suit almost every taste and every pocket. Amongst them are some of the finest of the world's wines, yet, by a process of classification, the quality varies down to the *vin rouge* enjoyed by the French labourer.

The wines of Burgundy

The very word Burgundy conjures up thoughts of Chablis, Beaune, Nuits St. Georges and Montrachet or Romanée. In the heart of the Burgundy region, running south from Dijon to the Beaujolais district north of Lyon, a wide range of red and white wines, both still and sparkling, is produced. These are almost entirely dry in character. The volume of red wine production is three times that of white.

The Burgundy range and variety is second only to that of Bordeaux, but, because of the inland climate, the Burgundies are generally bigger and fuller than the clarets, although not so long-lasting. In fact, the Mâconnais and Beaujolais wines are better drunk young, when they are fresh and fruity.

The Burgundy region is long and narrow. Going southeast from Paris, the first of the Burgundy districts is Chablis, where white wines of a remarkable freshness and flavour are made. Their rather dry and flinty character causes many to aver that they are the only wines to drink with shellfish. About sixty miles to the southeast of Chablis, the compact wine district known as the Côte d'Or begins. Here are the Côte de Nuits and the Côte de Beaune. In the middle of the Côte d'Or is the famous town of Beaune, known not only as a wine centre, but also for the Hospices de Beaune, which must rank among the most interesting buildings on the Continent. The Hospices, a charitable institution, was bequeathed a number of vineyards for its upkeep. Yearly sales of the Hospices wines, held in November each year, go back for many centuries. These wines are generally rather expensive, having regard to their charitable purpose, and are easily identified by their special label. However, the relationship between the prices fetched by the various Hospices wines gives a guide to Burgundy prices in the following year.

The Côte d'Or stretches from Dijon to Santenay, just north of Chalon-sur-Saône, and here the fine red and white Burgundies are made. The villages of Gevrey-Chambertin, Chambolle-Musigny, Vougeot, Vosne-Romanée and Nuits St. Georges produce some of the finest red wines of the Côte de Nuits. Equally famous, from the Côte de Beaune, are Aloxe-Corton, Beaune, Pommard and Volnay. At the southern end of the Côte de Beaune, fine white wines are made in Puligny-Montrachet and Meursault, names familiar throughout the world. In the Côte Chalonnaise are Mercurey and the Rully area, which produce fine red wines and wines suitable for conversion into sparkling Burgundy.

Some forty miles further south is Mâcon at the head of the Mâconnais and Beaujolais vineyards. Here the wines, though still classified as Burgundy, are somewhat lighter in texture and lack the body or fullness of a Vougeot or Meursault. Consequently, they tend to develop more quickly, and should be drunk young, for some of them are at their best when only a few months old, and make a fresh and fruity drink. In summer, the light red wines of the Beaujolais may, with advantage, be served cool, contrary to the usual practice. Generally, the red and white Mâcons are good value for money. Pouilly-Fuissé, a white wine without the delicacy of Chablis or the body of the Côte de Beaune white wines, is one of the best-known.

60

Fig. 14

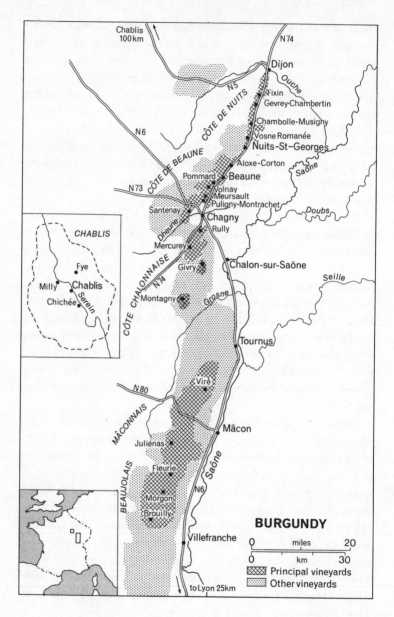

BURGUNDY

0   miles   20
0   km   30
▨ Principal vineyards
░ Other vineyards

The light red wines of Beaujolais may be sold under the district *Appellation* of Beaujolais or Beaujolais Supérieur; certain villages, however, are allowed to sell their wines under the name of their village as an *Appellation*, or where these village wines are blended together, under the name Beaujolais-Villages. Beaujolais wines can be made to keep and improve in bottle, when some of them will develop a character more like the wines of Mercurey.

The system of labelling the wines of Burgundy is logical and simple to follow. Firstly, a wide variety of wines may bear the name of the same village, even though produced in different qualities by different growers and at varying prices. Secondly, the villages or *communes* attach to their own name that of the most famous vineyard in their district. Thus Puligny (the village) attaches the name of Montrachet (the famous vineyard) and calls itself Puligny-Montrachet, as does the next village, Chassagne-Montrachet. There are many wines entitled to be called by their village names, but there is only one vineyard area which can produce wine to be labelled 'Le Montrachet', and of course this vineyard stretches over both villages.

Other French beverage wines

There are many worthy French wines produced outside the Bordeaux and Burgundy regions. The Rhône wines are a good example. Châteauneuf-du-Pape, Hermitage, and the Côtes-du-Rhône wines have earned a great reputation, possibly favouring red rather than white wines, and although fine white wines are made at Condrieu and St. Péray, they are seldom seen in England. The Rhône also produces the very popular rosé wine, Tavel Rosé.

Again, many good quality red, white and rosé wines may be found in the valley of the River Loire. They include very fine sweet wines from the Coteaux du Layon, a popular dry wine called Muscadet from vineyards at the mouth of the Loire, which is particularly suitable for the shellfish of that area, sparkling wines from Saumur and Vouvray and a range of rosé wines.

Fig. 15

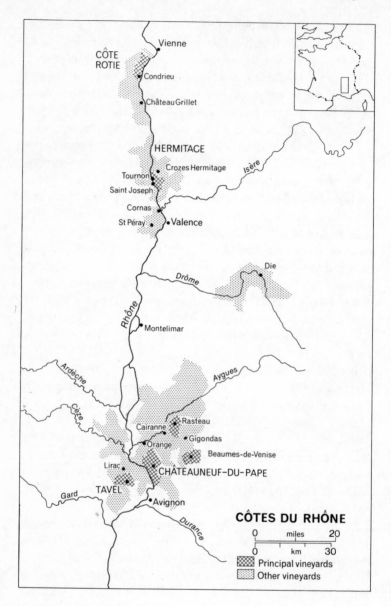

Vienne

CÔTE
ROTIE

Condrieu

Château Grillet

HERMITAGE

Crozes Hermitage

Isère

Tournon

Saint Joseph

Cornas

St Péray

Valence

Drôme

Die

Rhône

Montelimar

Ardèche

Aygues

Cèze

Cairanne

Rasteau

Orange

Gigondas

Beaumes-de-Venise

Lirac

CHÂTEAUNEUF–DU–PAPE

Gard

TAVEL

Avignon

Durance

CÔTES DU RHÔNE

0   miles   20

0   km   30

Principal vineyards

Other vineyards

Fig. 16

63

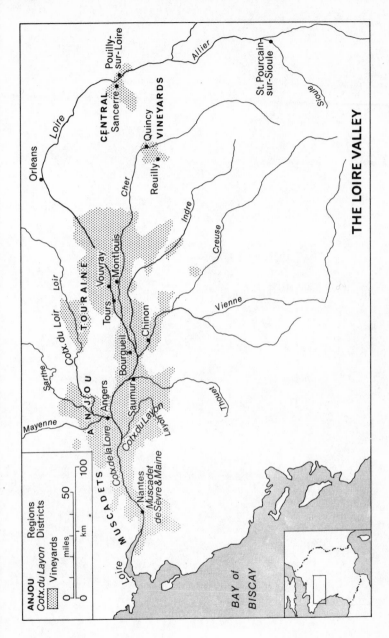

THE LOIRE VALLEY

ANJOU   Regions
Cotx.du Layon Districts
░░░ Vineyards

miles   0   50   100
km   0   50   100

CENTRAL VINEYARDS
Pouilly-sur-Loire
Sancerre
Quincy
Reuilly
St. Pourcain-sur-Sioule

Orleans
Loire
Allier
Sioule

TOURAINE
Vouvray
Montlouis
Tours
Chinon
Bourgueil
Cher
Indre
Creuse
Vienne

ANJOU
Angers
Saumur
Cotx.du Loir
Loir
Sarthe
Mayenne
Cotx.de la Loire
Cotx.du Layon
Layon
Thouet

MUSCADETS
Nantes
Muscadet de Sevre & Maine
Loire

BAY of BISCAY

Fig. 17

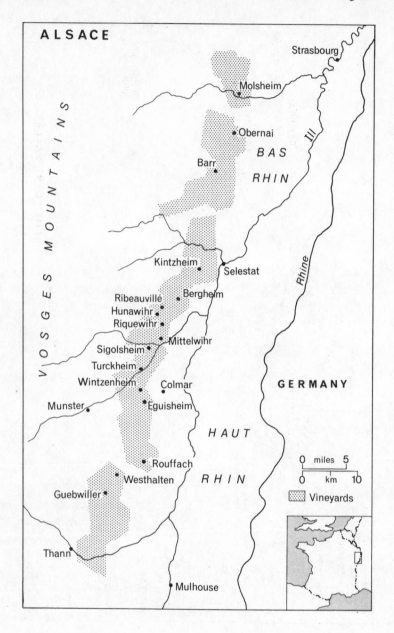

Opposite: A bunch of ripe Riesling grapes

Alsace is famed for wines akin to the German Hocks and Moselles; practically all are white wines, the majority being dry or medium-dry, although a good year may produce a sweet Alsatian wine. The Alsace wine label differs from other French wine labels inasmuch as the wines are named for the grape, the Riesling or Sylvaner for example, and not for the place-name, such as Beaune. The place-name can be added, however, as for example Riesling de Barr. The only controlled *Appellation* is 'Vin d'Alsace'. The best of the Alsace wines is probably Gewürztraminer, and bottles labelled Sylvaner, Pinot or Riesling are usually very good; a cheaper, blended wine is Zwicker. Generally, Alsatian wines need to be served cool and crisp, but not chilled excessively. In the summer they make a splendid thirst-quencher.

French wines come also from the Jura, Provence, the Midi and smaller scattered areas, but until now few of them have reached the export market. Their reputation among Englishmen has been restricted to those who have discovered them on their travels.

The wines of Germany

Germany is the producer of beverage wines ranking only second to France. In fact Germany is unsurpassed in her own white wine varieties, coming from the Rhine and Mosel valleys. Because the area of cultivation is almost at the northern limit of the wine belt, the growers are very much at the mercy of the weather. They have many difficulties with which to contend, so that production is comparatively small and the price reflects these difficulties. Practically all Rhine and Mosel wines have a magnificent bouquet and fine colouring. The rich Hocks, produced in limited quantity and only in good years, are among the world's most expensive wines.

Queen Victoria's favourite wine came from Hochheim in the Rheingau. The Queen used to visit the area frequently and she would say, 'Bring me a glass of *mein hock*', so that the name Hock came into the English language as describing Rhine wines in general.

Opposite: Harvesting the grapes

Hocks come mainly from four well-defined districts of the Rhine, extending from Coblenz to Mannheim: the Rheingau, Rheinhessen, Nahe and the Palatinate. Each district has its famous villages, giving their names to wine. From Rheingau come the wines of Rüdesheim, Johannisberg, Oestrich, Hattenheim, Erbach, Winkel, Kiedrich, and Hochheim. From Rheinhessen come the wines of Worms, (whose church, the Liebfrauenkirche, gave its name to 'Liebfraumilch'), Oppenheim, Nierstein and Nackenheim. The Nahe is the home of Schlossböckelheim, Niederhausen and Kreuznach wines, and from the Palatinate come the wines of Ruppertsberg, Deidesheim, Forst, Wachenheim, Dürkheim and Kallstadt.

These Rhine wines tend to be bigger, fuller and longer-lasting than the Mosel wines, which come from vineyards on the precipitous slate hills rising from the River Mosel and its tributaries, the Saar and Ruwer. The Moselles have a touch of acidity, derived from the soil as well as from their northern habitat, which makes them taste delightfully crisp and fresh when correctly chilled. They should be drunk when young.

The best-known wines from the Mosel valley are those of Trittenheim, Piesport, Brauneberg, Bernkastel, Graach, Wehlen, Zeltingen, Urzig and Traben-Trarbach. From the Saar, Ockfen, Wiltingen, Oberemmel and Ayl are among the finest names, and from the Ruwer, Casel.

Some red wines are made in Germany, but as red grapes need more warmth than white grapes to ripen satisfactorily, these red wines tend to be harsh, and are little-known outside Germany. Sparkling wines called Sekt or Schaumwein are also produced, and find a limited market in Great Britain.

Germany has a new wine law and quality control, intended both to guarantee the value of German wines and establish their identity. Government officials supervise both viticulture and vinification, and analysis of the wines in approved laboratories ensures that they conform with legal requirements. After examination in a laboratory, wines may be given an official

Fig. 18   67

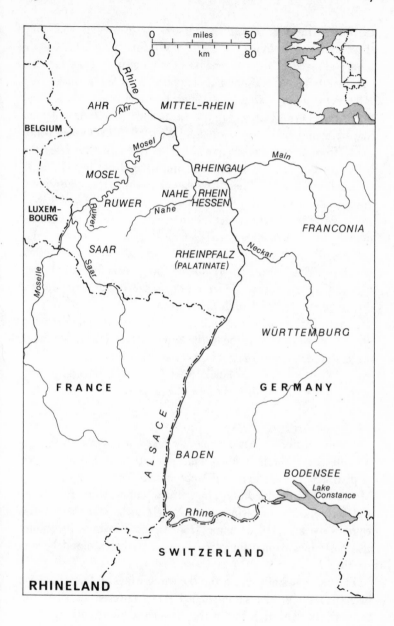

RHINELAND

certificate number (*Prüfungsnummer*), and are divided into three categories: *Deutscher Tafelwein* (table wine which is no longer allowed to bear the name of a vineyard), *Qualitätswein* (quality wine of designated region), or *Qualitätswein mit Prädikat* (quality wine with special attributes). Six special attributes (*Prädikaten*) can be awarded: *Kabinett*, elegant mature wines of superior quality; *Spätlese*, full-bodied wines made from late-gathered grapes left to ripen further after the main harvest; *Auslese*, noble aromatic wines from individually-selected bunches of grapes; *Beerenauslese*, wines from individual grapes which have been affected by 'noble rot'; *Trockenbeerenauslese*, the crowning achievement of German viticulture, made from raisin-like grapes shrivelled by noble rot, and comparable with the fine Sauternes; and *Eiswein*, a description which must be attached to one of the other five attributes, denoting a rare wine made from grapes harvested in the depths of winter and crushed while still frozen.

In addition, the label may indicate the vintage, the vineyard, the grape variety and the name of the 'wine-grower'. With a patient understanding of all these disciplines, the wine-lover can learn much from German wine labels. Such knowledge can add greatly to the enjoyment of a broad range of beautiful wines.

The wines of Italy

The wine regions of Italy generally take their names from the provinces, and the individual wines are either named for grapes or districts. The Barbera and Nebbiolo red wines and the white Moscato, all from Piedmont, have grape names, while Bardolino and Valpolicella, red wines from Lake Garda, and the famous white Soave are all place-names from Veneto province. Piedmont also has wines named for places – Asti, Barbaresco and Barolo are three.

The red wines of Chianti and the white wines of Tuscany have been put up in the same-shaped straw-covered flasks down through the centuries, but in the modern economy this bottle is

Fig. 19

69

becoming too expensive to survive. This applies also to the dry (*secco*) and sweet (*abboccato*) white wines of Orvieto. None of these wines will suffer from a conventional shape of bottle. Indeed, legislation in Italy during the last few years gives the consumer a far greater guarantee of quality than he has ever enjoyed in Italy's 2700 years of wine-making.

Beverage wines of high standard are produced in most of the countries bordering the Mediterranean – Greece, Turkey, Cyprus, Malta and North Africa – and from Australia, South Africa, California and several of the South American countries, particularly Chile, Brazil and Argentina. However, much of their wine is drunk locally and little has hitherto been available for export.

The important thing to remember is that individual grape varieties have their own characteristics which come out strongly in the wine. Another reason why the wine of one château in the Médoc differs from that produced by a neighbour is that each is planted with various vines in differing proportions and of different ages, and this applies to wines the world over. Furthermore the constituents of the soil and the distribution of sunshine and rainfall vary, and even the configuration of the land has its effect. There is no standard vineyard or universal grape. If there were, perhaps wine would lose much of its magic.

Sparkling wines

Very occasionally a discovery of great importance can make a significant contribution to civilization. For the wine trade, the discovery of the principle of secondary fermentation during the early eighteenth century was such an event. For many centuries an inferior cloudy wine that bubbled had been known, but soon wine was to sparkle with crystal clarity. By definition, a sparkling wine is one where natural gas from fermentation is retained in the bottle, or one where the wine has been artificially impregnated with gas. An unofficial UK Customs definition of sparkling wine is 'a wine with a wired cork'.

The discovery of sparkling wines coincided with the first use of corks, and it was noticed, particularly in the northern parts of Europe, that in the springtime certain of the wines were given to popping their corks. These were called 'devil wines'. It is now obvious that some sort of fermentation must have been taking place in the bottle, although this fermentation did not necessarily leave any sediment. As it did not leave a sediment, and these were dry wines, it could not have been the normal fermentation of sugar to form alcohol and carbon dioxide. It is now known that the fermentation was due to a changing in the acids of the wine. One of the most important fruit acids is malic acid, found in apples, and as drinkers of rough cider will know, it is very acid indeed. This malic acid is attacked by minute organisms, particularly at the time of the year when the sap is rising, and turned into lactic acid, which takes its name from milk and is a much softer acid. In this process carbon dioxide is created, so that after this malo-lactic fermentation the wine becomes less acid and slightly sparkling, or *pétillant* as they say in France. This can be enough to make the usual beverage wine cork pop out of the bottle, letting the wine escape.

This phenomenon was particularly evident in the cold northern land of Champagne, where the monks of the Abbey of Haut-villers studied it carefully. They concluded that if they had stronger bottles and tighter corks the bubbles could be contained. They put their theory into practice and the wine became popular. It also occurred to the monks that if a little extra sugar and yeast were added to the still wine before bottling, a stronger fermentation would give the wine even more sparkle.

The must for sparkling wine, wherever and however made, is fermented naturally and completely to produce a still white wine. It is quite probable that the making of Champagne originated in the fact that in northern climates it is very cold just after the harvest, and therefore difficult to keep fermentation of the must going. This 'stuck' fermentation will normally restart in the spring if the winter has not been too cold, and will continue until all the sugar has been converted, although some yeast will have been lost.

The cellar master of Hautvillers at this time (the year 1700) was Dom Pérignon, and in Reims may be seen a statue erected to his memory, for he is regarded as the 'Father of Champagne'. Although he may not have invented the process which led to the second fermentation, he undoubtedly perfected the system of blending the wines together.

However, the addition of sugar and yeast to the wine before bottling had one unfortunate corollary. Besides producing extra carbon dioxide and a little extra alcohol, it also produced a mass of dead yeast cells. In the first fermentation, dead yeast cells are normally left in the cask or vat when the wine is racked from them, but when they are in bottle under a pressure that must not be lost, it is more difficult to get rid of them. For many years people grew accustomed to drinking the wine of Champagne in a cloudy, yeasty condition – not at all like the Champagne of today.

Methods of production
Since Dom Pérignon's discovery, four methods of making a clear sparkling wine have been developed – the Champagne method,

Fig. 20   73

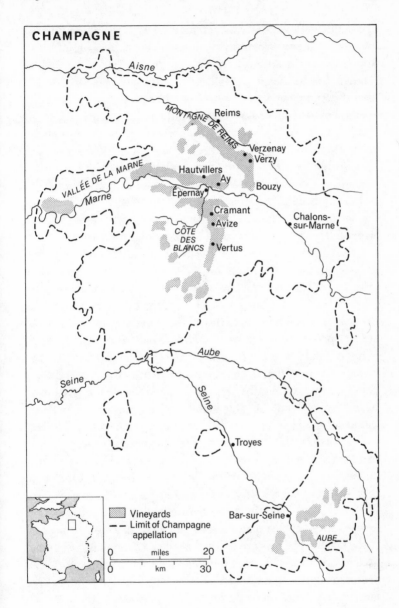

CHAMPAGNE

Aisne

MONTAGNE DE REIMS
Reims
Verzenay
Verzy

VALLÉE DE LA MARNE
Hautvillers
Ay
Bouzy
Épernay
Marne
Cramant
Avize
Chalons-sur-Marne
CÔTE DES BLANCS
Vertus

Aube

Seine

Seine

Troyes

Vineyards
Limit of Champagne appellation

Bar-sur-Seine
AUBE

miles   20
km   30

the tank method, the transfer method and the impregnation method. All four systems may be used in the making of other sparkling wines, but only the Champagne method is allowed by French law in the production of Champagne. And by French law 'Champagne' means wine produced by the Champagne method in the Champagne region, and no other. Indeed England has recently established the same restrictions to the use of the name Champagne.

The four methods of making sparkling wines fall into two categories. The first three are natural, with a second fermentation, maturation, and removal of the sediment; the fourth is artificial, carbon dioxide gas being injected into a vat of still wine, and the gasified wine then bottled under pressure.

The Champagne method comes first, and undoubtedly this method produces the finest sparkling wine. Exactly four tons of grapes are placed in a Champagne press, where they are pressed three times. It is not an essential part of the Champagne method, but it is an essential part of the making of Champagne, that this type of press should be used, and that only a limited quantity of must should be taken from the grapes.

After fermentation the wine is racked in the usual way and after about four to five months, depending upon the area, it is ready to be made sparkling. At this stage in the Champagne method, liquid sugar and yeast are added to the wine in carefully measured quantities, and the wine is then bottled in special strong bottles, and corked firmly with the cork clamped down. The cork bulges out like a mushroom above the head of the bottle, because it is much bigger than the neck of the bottle and has had to be forced in. There is a 'V' cut in the top of the cork to locate the clip or *agrafe* which fits over it and is secured under the ridge in the neck of the bottle. The modern method of crown corking is now being used in Champagne as elsewhere, and is perfectly satisfactory and acceptable. After the mixture of wine, sugar and yeast has been bottled and tightly corked, the bottles are taken down to a cool cellar – about 10°C (50°F) – and are laid on their sides.

The fermentation proceeds just as the first one did. The yeast turns the sugar into carbon dioxide and ethyl alcohol but, unlike the first fermentation, the carbon dioxide cannot escape and becomes dissolved in the wine. This creates a considerable pressure of about 65 pounds per square inch (similar to the pressure in the tyres of a double-decker bus). So the bottles have to be extremely strong and the corks clamped very firmly. In the old days, when there was uncertainty about the quantities of sugar and yeast to add, there were many breakages during fermentation, and the men who attended the bottles in the cellars were paid danger money. Now, with the benefit of the scientist François's device to measure the exact amount of sugar, and the use of uniformly and strongly made bottles, breakages are rare.

The bottles stay binned on their sides until the second fermentation is complete, which may take up to six months. Every few weeks they are taken up, shaken, and put down in a slightly different position, so that the sediment does not stick to any particular part of the inside of the bottle. When this ripening period is completed, the process of removing the sediment begins. In the Champagne method this is done by a process called *remuage*, which means shaking, developed by the Widow Clicquot in about 1800.

The object of *remuage* is to remove the sediment in the bottle on to the cork. It might be asked why the bottles were not stacked upside down in the first place, so that the sediment would naturally fall on to the cork. The answer is that the sediment is of two types: first, a heavy granular sediment is formed; then, as the fermentation proceeds, the sediment becomes finer and is more easily disturbed. The art is to get this fine sediment to go down on to the cork first, so that the heavier granular sediment can sit on top of it and thus prevent it from clouding the wine, which it would otherwise do every time the bottle was moved in the slightest degree. Fig. 21 shows the oval holes in the *pupitre* or rack, which is so constructed that a bottle may be held quite firmly in the nearly-horizontal or the nearly-vertical position, as

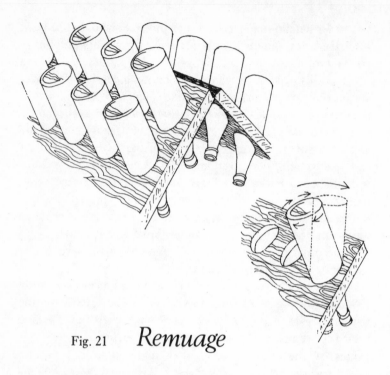

Fig. 21   *Remuage*

the bottle shows. Each day the *remueur*, who is a very skilled man, gives each bottle a little shake and a slight twist. It is a most dexterous operation, difficult to perform. Nevertheless, after a long and arduous apprenticeship, a skilled *remueur* can treat 30,000 bottles every day. It is therefore a very expensive operation, which the Americans have been trying to mechanize, apparently with some success.

As the *remueur* shakes each bottle each day, he tilts it gradually, degree by degree, from the horizontal up to the vertical. After two or three months the sediment will have moved down to lie on the cork. The first stage of removing the sediment has now been finished, and the wine is put aside for ageing. The bottles are stacked very carefully so that the cork of each rests in the hollow of the bottom of the one below, thus ensuring that the sediment remains on the cork. For Champagne, the legal minimum period of ageing is one year, but most Champagnes are aged for at least three years.

The bottles resting *en masse*, as they say in Champagne, may however stay there for a very long time; the wine will go to sleep and mature until it is wanted. No matter for how long it ages, the second stage of eliminating sediment must ensue. This process, known as *dégorgement* in France, consists of getting all the sediment out of the bottle, without losing the wine.

By the old-fashioned, manual process, the bottles were taken upside down to the *dégorgeur*, who skilfully removed the *agrafe* while holding the cork in position, and then eased the cork out of the bottle, at the same time bringing the bottle upright. The pressure in the bottle forced the sediment with the cork out of the bottle. After a quick sniff to ensure all the sediment was gone and the wine clean, the bottle was replenished and recorked with a new cork held down by a wire muzzle. A little sugar was usually added to the replenishing wine, to sweeten the product to the extent required by the market. This was the traditional method of *dégorgement* and was occasionally a little wasteful of wine.

Nowadays an automatic procedure is available, in which the bottles are brought from the cellar upside down and immersed in a bath of chilled brine, so that the quarter inch of wine above the cork freezes. In this pellet of ice all the sediment is imprisoned. The cork can then be taken off (a crown cork can be removed automatically), when pressure in the bottle expels the pellet of ice, and the bottle topped up, recorked and shipped out, in the knowledge that it is sound. A special machine adds the little sugared *dosage* to the bottle, to bring it up to the market sweetness required.

There are several styles of sparkling wine, the driest of which is Brut or Natur and the sweetest Rich or Doux; the percentage of sugar syrup in the *dosage* which is added varies from nil – filling up with just plain wine – to filling up with wine that has been mixed with 10% of sugar syrup. This mixture of wine and sugar is shaken up with the rest of the wine under pressure in the bottle, either by hand or by a machine which gently turns the bottles over and over. The bottles are then put down into the cellars again so that the liqueur can 'marry' with the wine. Finally the bottles are brought up for labelling and capsuling with gold foil, after which they are ready for marketing.

Sparkling wine comes in many different sizes of bottle, ranging from the quarter bottle up to the Nebuchadnezzar, holding the equivalent of twenty bottles. These two ends of the scale would be quite impossible to clarify by *remuage*; the quarter bottle would be too trifling to handle, while the loss from a burst twenty-bottle Nebuchadnezzar would be too great. So, it is normal to bottle in the ordinary-size bottle of 28 fluid ounces (80 centilitres) and to a certain extent in half bottles or in magnums, equivalent to two bottles. For larger and smaller-sized bottles, the wine is withdrawn from the original bottle after *dégorgement* and is then filled into the appropriate bottle under pressure, so that none of the sparkle is lost. Obviously for this purpose the

SPARKLING WINE STYLES		Table 1
Style	**Equivalent**	**Liqueur %**
BRUT, NATUR	Very Dry	0—2
EXTRA DRY, EXTRA SEC, TRÈS SEC	Dry	2—3
SEC	Medium Dry	4—5
DEMI-SEC	Medium Sweet	7—9
RICH, DOUX	Very Sweet	9—10

magnum would be a more efficient size, as the *remuage* and *dégorgement* could be done at twice the speed of the single bottle.

Curiously, the wine coming from the magnum seems to be better than that which is made in the ordinary bottle. So much so that a scientist named Charmat conceived the sealed tank method to get rid of the sediment more easily and cheaply. After carrying out the second fermentation in a closed tank it was possible to filter the wine under pressure, so that the sediment was left behind, and then to bottle the wine, still under pressure. The French term *cuve close*, often appearing on wine labels, simply means 'closed tank'. It was found that this method did not make such a fine sparkling wine, and the French Government ruled that it could not be used for Champagne or for any sparkling wine bearing *Appellation Contrôlée*. However, this method is widely used in other countries.

The Champagne method is expensive because it involves so much work by skilled craftsmen. The tank method, being less labour-intensive, allows sparkling wine to be made more cheaply. The sparkle lacks the permanence of the Champagne method, however, the bubbles usually being larger and not remaining in the wine so long. So a compromise was sought to maintain the excellence of the Champagne method and the cheapness of the tank method. This resulted in the third method shown in Fig. 22, page 80, the transfer method.

Here the second fermentation takes place in bottles and the wine is matured or ripened lying down in cellars just as in the Champagne method, but at this point the method changes. Instead of undergoing the expensive *remuage* and *dégorgement* processes, the bottles are taken, very cold, straight to the point of disgorgement. As soon as the corks are removed the sediment rises up in the wine and clouds it. All this clouded wine is then sucked out of the bottle through a filter; and after the addition of a *dosage*, the filtered wine is pumped, still under pressure, into clean bottles of the size required, which are then firmly corked and muzzled. The apparatus for this looks remarkably like an

SPARKLING WINES		
(A)	2nd Fermentation and Maturation	Clearance of Sediment
Champagne method	In Bottle	Remuage and Dégorgement
Tank method (Cuve Close)	In Tank	Filtration
Transfer method	In Bottle	Vatting under pressure, then Filtration
(B) **Carbonation** (Gazefié)	Carbon Dioxide (CO_2) injected into chilled vat of still wine, which is then bottled under pressure. Much cheaper.	

automatic *dégorgement* and liqueuring machine in Champagne, or the machine that withdraws wine from the Champagne magnums to fill them into smaller or larger-sized bottles. The difference is that the wine taken out of bottles in the transfer method contains sediment which has to be filtered out. It is possible to confuse the transfer of cleared wine in the Champagne method, with the transfer, filtering and rebottling of clouded wine in the transfer method. Certainly, the transfer method may not be used for any quality wine in France, although it may be used for quality wines elsewhere.

Finally, in the carbonation method, the wine is cooled to a very low temperature in a closed vat, so that frost forms on the outside. A special apparatus injects carbon dioxide gas into the still, chilled wine, and the wine is then bottled under pressure. Wine made by this method is not so much sparkling as 'sparkled'. When the cork is removed, the bubbles will very soon disappear, just as they do from an open bottle of artificial soda-water or fizzy orangeade.

Opposite: Top – Casks in Champagne Chai; Bottom – Champagne press after the first crushing of the grapes

Sparkling wines are nearly always white, although there are a few pink ones. Sparkling red wine *can* be found, but it should be remembered that red wines tend to throw a deposit in bottle, and that sparkling wines cannot be decanted as still wines can. Just as white wines generally have a shorter life than red, so do sparkling wines; as a rule, they will have a maximum life of ten years after *dégorgement* and recorking, but there have been notable exceptions due to superlative vinification, corking and storage.

Champagne

Not all wines made by the Champagne method are Champagne, yet Champagne is acknowledged as being the finest of them all. Why should this be? Consider the main factors which determine the quality of production in Champagne. The grapes used are the Pinot Noir and the Pinot Meunier; yet these grapes, with the Chardonnay, are also used in other areas to make sparkling wines. So the answer must lie in two other factors, the climate and the soil.

The Champagne region is generally divided into three areas, the Montagne de Reims, which lends backbone or a framework to the wine, the Vallée de la Marne, which gives it bouquet, and the Côte des Blancs, where the wine is made entirely from the white Chardonnay grape, adding finesse. Sometimes the wine from the Côte des Blancs is marketed on its own as 'Blanc de Blancs' – a white wine from white grapes – but this wine is too light and delicate for popularity.

The Champagne region lies northeast of Paris, and being some 200 miles inland, has a more continental climate than the maritime provinces, having colder winters and hotter summers. The soil of Champagne, below a thin topsoil, is pure chalk, similar to that found in the North and South Downs of England. Calcareous soils, chalk and limestone, always accentuate the flavour of the grape in the wine. Moreover, in this most northerly French vineyard region, every calorie of heat in summer is important: this is stored up in the chalk soil during the day, as in a

Opposite: Bunnahabhain Distillery

night-storage heater. The heat is then transmitted anew to the vines and grapes at night, enabling them to continue ripening.

Although the viticultural methods used are similar to those used in other areas, in Champagne greater care is necessary and indeed is exercised. When it comes to the time of the vintage, all unripe and rotten grapes, and those which have been damaged by hail, are cut out. So also with the vinification: of each charge of four tons of grapes in the press, only ten barrels, amounting to 220 gallons (2000 litres) are taken for the finest wines. After the first pressing, which yields this amount, the press is raised, the grapes are broken up, and then again pressed to give a further one and a half barrels of must. This process is repeated once more, but the must produced by these two *tailles* is not used for the finest Champagnes. Finally, the mass of grapes, which still contains much juice, is pressed harshly to produce the *rebêche*, which is usually used for local drinking and for the making of the very fine *marc de Champagne*.

One factor which has not yet been mentioned is luck. Luck is particularly important in northern climes; for until the harvest is gathered, the wine fermented, and the blending done, it is not known whether the wine will make a Vintage Champagne. And even in years which produce wines fine enough to stand on their own with their year's name, it is not certain whether there will be sufficient yield to allow it to be marketed as such. Fine wine is too valuable to the wine-maker for improving the quality of his normal blended wines in poorer years, for him easily to allow himself the luxury of declaring a Vintage.

Other sparkling wines

None of the other sparkling wines of France which are entitled to the *Appellation Contrôlée* are as famous as Champagne. From the Loire there is Saumur and Vouvray, both with *Appellation*. From Burgundy there is sparkling Burgundy, also with AC, and much good sparkling wine made by other methods and therefore sold under trade names; these latter are often good value for money and worthy of appreciative drinking. In Bordeaux much sparkling wine is made, but all by the tank method, thus lacking the *Appellation Contrôlée*. There are other AC sparkling wines in France, but few of them come to England, and are, so far, of little account to the British market.

The Champagne method is very expensive in manpower, while the tank and transfer methods are expensive in equipment. Therefore the *méthode Champenoise* is to be expected in countries where labour is relatively cheap, such as Spain: many good wines are made by the Champagne method in Catalonia and Rioja, although they lack the finesse of Champagne.

Other sparkling wines worthy of mention include Asti Spumante, from the little town of Asti near Turin in Northern Italy, made by the tank method from the Muscatel grape, and having a Denominazione di Origine Controllata; and the German wines, Deutscher Sekt, Deutscher Prädikat Sekt and Schaumwein, made by different methods and all entitled to quality labels.

Russia has a 'Champagne' from Georgia, and the USA also produces 'Champagnes'; the laws of these countries do not require that this term be used only for the wine of France, although Canadian law does so.

In a sentence, there are many sparkling wines, but there is only one Champagne.

Fortified wines

Fortified wines have a greater proportion of alcohol than beverage wines, because they have been strengthened or fortified with spirit during manufacture. Beverage wines have a strength of between 9% and 18% of alcohol, whereas fortified wines have a strength of between 17% and 24%. The added spirit is usually, but not always, local brandy made from wine. The brandy has an affinity with the wine, and is also cheap because surplus wine is always available in the vineyards for distillation into spirit. Substandard wine can also be used, as for instance the lees of the wine, and wine from the last pressing of the grapes.

Fortified wines may be of many types; they may be sweet or dry, they may be red, white, rosé or brown, they may be given a special flavour. They are produced in many parts of the world, in any area where wine and brandy can be made.

The two most important fortified wines come from the Iberian Peninsula. These are sherry and port, each made in a distinctive way; their methods of fortification are classic, and the 'sherry method' and 'port method' are used in a variety of other fortified wines.

In the sherry method the spirit is added *after the wine has fermented to dryness and consumed all the sugar of the grape.* The group of fortified wines made by this method includes the original Spanish sherry, the 'sherries' made in Australia, South Africa, Cyprus and Britain, Vermouths and some Madeiras.

In the port method the spirit is added *during fermentation in sufficient quantity to arrest fermentation.* When the alcoholic strength is raised above the level at which the yeast can continue to work, the natural sugars cease to be converted into alcohol, and the wine is left sweet. Some Madeiras, and the sweet wines of southern France called *vins doux naturels* (natural sweet wines),

Fig. 23

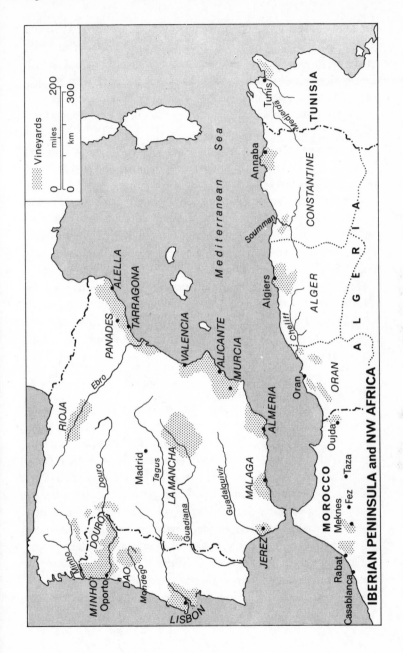

are made in this way. These are mostly made from the Muscatel grape. What are called *mistelles* in France, or *mistellas* in Italy, such as Pineau des Charentes, are not strictly wines at all, being merely grape juice which has been fortified with brandy before it has a chance to start fermentation at all. They can be distinguished from wine because they taste of grape juice and not of wine.

The names of sherry and port are protected by law in the United Kingdom, sherry because of civil cases and port because of treaties, ratified by Act of Parliament.

Although the name 'sherry', on its own, describes a wine which must come from Spain, a label showing, for instance, 'Australian Sherry', is legal in the United Kingdom provided that the words 'Australian' and 'Sherry' are of the same size, and immediately next to each other.

The word 'port' is strongly protected, in that it may not be used by itself to describe *any* other wine. The Australians make a wine similar to port which they may call 'port style' or 'port type', but they may not call it port and the label may not show, for instance, 'Australian Port'.

Sherry

The sherry country is the Jerez region of Spain, and is shown in Fig. 24. The name 'Jerez' in modern Spanish derives from the Moorish 'Sherris', recognizable from the works of Shakespeare. Although Jerez de la Frontera is the centre of the region, there are some other important towns which are noteworthy for sherry. Sherry is shipped around the world from the port of Cadiz and from Port de St. Marie, the little port from which Columbus sailed to discover the Americas. Another important village to the north of the region is Sanlucar de Barrameda, noted for one particular wine, Manzanilla, which gains its peculiar salty quality from maturation by the sea.

Different shadings in Fig. 24 denote Albariza, Barros and Arenas soils, which have an important effect in this region.

Fig. 24   87

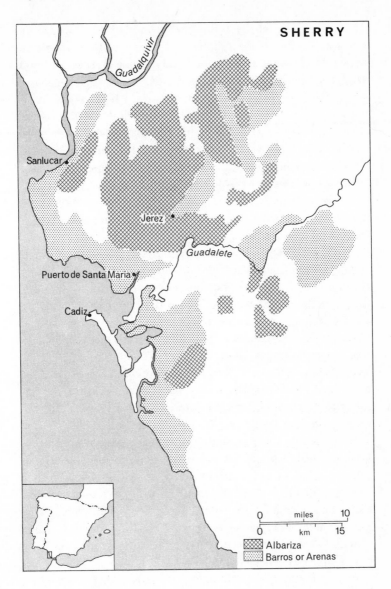

SHERRY

Guadalquivir

Sanlucar

Jerez

Guadalete

Puerto de Santa Maria

Cadiz

| 0 | miles | 10 |
| 0 | km | 15 |

Albariza
Barros or Arenas

Albariza is a very chalky soil, rather crumbly but gummy in the wet season, due to the presence of clay. The Barros soils are darker in colour and have more clay, while Arenas are more sandy; neither produce quite such fine wines, as the Albariza soil contains a greater proportion of chalk, which always accentuates the flavour of the grape. This very white soil also reflects the sunlight brilliantly, helping to ripen the grapes.

The grapes used for sherry are the Palomino, the Pedro Ximenes and the Muscatel. The Palomino is the most important, Pedro Ximenes and Muscatel being used for sweetening only.

In the modern scene, baskets for collecting the grapes are giving way to plastic containers which are lighter and easier to keep clean, besides being less expensive.

As the Jerez region is so hot, the grapes develop a great deal of sugar. This sugar is sometimes further concentrated by laying the grapes on mats in the hot sun, but covering them very carefully at night against the dew. This is done in order to evaporate some of the water, and thus increase the concentration of sugar in the grape. Nevertheless, a hot climate means that there will be less acid in the grapes, and wine must have sufficient acid if it is to have a balanced flavour. Therefore, before the grapes are trodden or pressed, they are 'plastered' – that is to say gypsum, the raw material of plaster of Paris, is scattered over the grapes. This will react to produce tartaric acid to balance the wine.

When ready, the Palomino grapes are taken to large warehouses called *bodegas* for pressing. Traditionally the grapes were trodden in open shallow troughs called *lagares*, which were usually about twelve feet square, with sides some two feet high. The men wore traditional Jerez boots with nails driven into the soles at angles so as to avoid crushing the pips, which contain bitter oils. When they had crushed the grapes, the juice ran off and was collected.

In this method, the soft pulp residue is gathered up into a pyramid around the screw in the middle of the *lagar* and long, plaited grass lanyards are wound round, covering it completely.

A plate is put on top and screwed down so that more juice can be pressed out of the grapes. This pressing operation is repeated two or three times, but the juice from the later pressings is only used for making brandy. The *lagar* is now largely superseded by modern rotary presses, which extract the juice without danger of the grape pips being crushed.

The juice or *mosto* runs from the *lagares* or presses into vats or barrels, where it ferments furiously for three or four days. The fermentation continues more quietly for about another three weeks, until the yeast has consumed all the sugar, leaving a still white wine. This wine is run off its lees into casks, called butts; confusingly, this new wine is known as *mosto*. The wine is left to mature in the casks without the bungs on and without topping up. At this stage the first fortification is made, bringing the alcoholic strength up to about 15%. During this first stage of maturation, an important development in the making of sherry takes place.

On some casks, quite at random, a substance known as *flor* forms. Flor is a yeast, rather like cream cheese in appearance, which floats on the surface of the wine. The casks being open, the aerobic *flor* can take oxygen from the air and feed on the wine itself. In the process, it changes the flavour of the wine, while also increasing the alcoholic strength slightly. It may be that, of two casks filled with must at the same time from the same press, one will grow *flor* and the other will not.

At this stage the *catador* or taster comes on the scene. With the help of the *venenciador*, who inserts a *venencia* (a small cup on the end of a long whalebone stick) through the bunghole to gather a sample of *mosto*, the *catador* tastes, or rather noses, the sample from each barrel and classifies it. Those which have *flor* are classified as *finos* and their casks are cut with a Y-shaped mark called a *palma*. Those which do not are classified as *rayas* and are marked with a stroke or *raya*.

Fig. 25 shows the family tree of sherry, with *mosto* at the top, and the first important classification into *finos* and *rayas*. On the

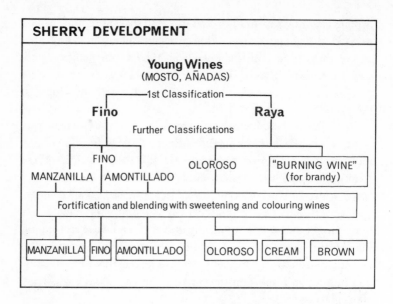

SHERRY DEVELOPMENT

Young Wines
(MOSTO, AÑADAS)

────1st Classification────

Fino   **Raya**

Further Classifications

FINO
MANZANILLA   AMONTILLADO   OLOROSO   "BURNING WINE"
                                          (for brandy)

Fortification and blending with sweetening and colouring wines

MANZANILLA FINO AMONTILLADO   OLOROSO   CREAM   BROWN

fino side, from the casks which have developed *flor*, will be seen Fino itself, a well-known style of sherry, and in addition Manzanilla and Amontillado. If Fino is matured at Sanlucar de Barrameda, near the sea, it will acquire a salty tang which is readily distinguishable as a separate style, known as Manzanilla. Finos kept for a long time will become what the trade calls 'fat' – slightly darker in colour and fuller in flavour, with a pleasant nutty tang. These are called Amontillados. Their name derives from the wines of similar character produced at Montilla near Cordoba, which were greatly sought after before Jerez became famous. The Montilla wines were so popular that the people of Jerez called their wines 'Amontillado' – 'like the wines of Montilla'.

On the *raya* side of the figure, the wines develop into Olorosos, or alternatively are relegated into 'wines for burning'. Wines left open to the air do not generally do well, and can easily turn sour. *Flor* protects the *finos* from this fate because it covers the surface of the wines, but *rayas* do not have this advantage. Some are strong enough to stand it and develop into Olorosos, but some go bad. These are immediately detected by classification and testing, and are put aside to be made into brandy, hence the name 'wines for burning'.

The chart shows expansion of the Olorosos into different styles of sherry, entirely due to blending with other wines. Another sherry type called *palo cortado* is occasionally found. This is a very rare wine, an Oloroso which develops Fino characteristics, and is usually very expensive.

There are no vintages in sherry. All sherries are blends of many years and the blending is done by a special method known as the *solera* system. The wines start by being all of one year, and remain so in their individual butts for several years, until they have decided whether they are going to become Finos or Olorosos. Very few *rayas* manage to become *finos*. It is usual after the first classification for a further fortification to be given to the *rayas*. They cannot then become *finos*, because *flor* will not stand a percentage of alcohol above 18%. Even within the broad classifications of Fino and Raya, there will be very different characteristics: individual butts will assume different qualities, just as members of a family may resemble each other very closely or may be quite different. The *catador's* task is to categorize each butt frequently, so that he can see which of his standard *soleras* it resembles most. He keeps all the different styles in different casks.

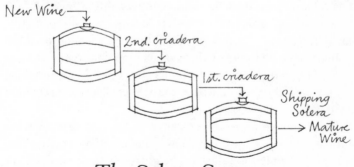

Fig. 26   *The Solera System*

It is a characteristic of sherry that if a small amount of similar, although younger, wine is added to a large amount of older wine, the younger wine will gradually take on the characteristics of the older, rather as children learn from their elders at school. In fact the Spaniards think of it this way – they put each wine from its *añada* stage (wine of a single year) to its appropriate nursery school, called a *criadera* (reminiscent of a nursery) after which it progresses through successive stages. Just as children move up their school as they develop, so the wines from the *criaderas* progress through the scales of the *solera*. A *solera* consists of a variable number of casks arranged in scales. To give an idea of how the system works, imagine six scales, the first consisting of 40 or 50 butts. The wine from the first scale is the one ready to be sold. This scale is often known as the 'shipping *solera*'. The scale backing it up has an equal number of butts of wine about a year younger, and so on until the sixth and last scale, where the wine will be about five years younger than that of the first. When wine is drawn from a butt in the first scale, this butt will be replenished with equal quantities from each of the butts in the second scale. These butts in turn will be similarly replenished from the butts in the third scale, replenished in their turn from the fourth, and so on until the sixth, which is replenished from the *añada*.

Because wine changes as it matures, it varies in quality from year to year, usually acquiring more strength, body and colour. The *solera* system tends to compensate for this change. But the system will only work if the transfers of wine are made gradually, one jar at a time. A jarful is 'called' through a siphon from the younger scale and poured through a funnel into the next older scale. The funnel used for 'running the scales' has a very long spout so that the wine may be introduced at all levels throughout the butt.

The Palomino grape is the source of *fino* and *raya* sherries, but two other varieties, the Pedro Ximenes and the Muscatel, have very definite usefulness. The grapes of these varieties are usually left to dry in the sun for two or three weeks so that they become quite shrivelled and very sweet; they are then fermented normally to produce a very sweet wine of low alcoholic content, for excessive sugar inhibits fermentation. Wines for sale in cold northern climates need sweetening to be acceptable, and we know that the *solera* wines are all bone dry. So the sweet wine obtained from the Pedro Ximenes and Muscatel grapes is added to the dry wine before shipment. Again, wines from different butts may vary greatly in colour, but the final blends must be identical in colour to previous shipments. To achieve this, 'colouring wine' or *vino de color*, is added. This is made from the fermentation of one part of unfermented must with two parts of grape syrup obtained by boiling down grape juice until it caramelizes. The blend ferments slowly and, when it has been aged in cask, a highly aromatic and very dark *vino de color* is obtained. This looks rather like gravy browning, and is in fact the best possible basis for a brown sauce.

When the sherry shipper receives an order for a particular brand for one customer or another, he will look up his blending book, take the wines he needs from his shipping *soleras*, and blend them, together with sweetening wine and *vino de color*.

The sherry *soleras* are housed in *bodegas*, which are above ground. With high roofs and thick walls, they have been designed to maintain a temperature exactly suited to the maturation of sherry. Stainless steel vats are also used in the *soleras*, not for maturing sherry, but for conditioning the final blend prior to shipment. The final blend, which has also to be fortified up to shipping strength with more brandy, is placed in these vats and refrigerated. This is done to precipitate tartrates and other soluble salts, so that the wine may thereafter keep clear and bright in all conditions.

Port

The other great fortified wine is port, which comes from the Douro valley in the north of Portugal. The town of Porto, often

called Oporto (the 'O' meaning 'the'), is on the north bank of
the mouth of the Douro river; across the river is its suburb,
Vila Nova de Gaia. The port wine brought down from the vineyards must by Portuguese law be stored here for its maturation.
Some forty miles up the Douro from Porto is the town of Regua,
in the middle of the most productive district of the Douro valley.
The port-producing region of the Upper Douro extends up
the river to the Spanish border. But although the Douro rises
well within Spain, near to Madrid, nothing like port is produced
from its vineyards outside Portugal.

The country is very mountainous and rises steeply from the
twisting river. This region has very cold wet winters with some
fifty inches of rain, considerably more than in the United
Kingdom. But in the summer it is hot and dry. The steep
mountainsides guarding the river have to be terraced, to make
reasonably flat areas for growing the vine. This creates continual
work, especially as the torrential winter rains wash much soil to
the bottom of the valley, whence it must be carried up again.
Olives are planted among the vines to help hold the slaty soil
together. The vines grow below the critical 400-metre line,
above which grapes may not be used for port. Even below the
400-metre line only a proportion of the grapes is allowed to be
used; they must be very carefully chosen, the remainder being
used for light beverage wines.

Several grapes are used for making port, contrasting with
sherry which is almost entirely made from one grape, the
Palomino. The vines grow in schistous soil, which is sometimes
so hard that pickaxes cannot break it, and explosives have to be
used to make holes for new vines. When the grapes are picked
they are taken to the nearby wineries of the *quintas*, where they
enter the press house. By traditional method, the grapes are put
into a *lagar* as for sherry; but in this case, the *lagar* is stopped,
that is to say the juice is not allowed to run off as the pressing
continues, but is left in the *lagar*. The grapes for port are fermented on their skins, and therefore most of them are of the

Fig. 27   95

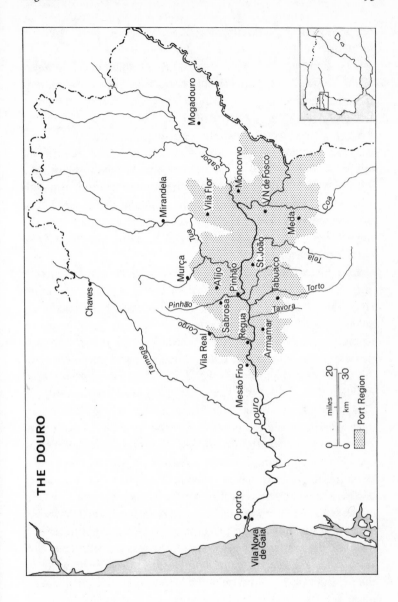

THE DOURO

black varieties, producing a red wine. White ports are also fermented on their skins, unlike sherries.

The treading was previously a test of manhood, the *lagar* of the Douro being rather deeper than that of Jerez, and indeed treading grapes was a very hard job. The heat of the body helped to accelerate the fermentation. When enough colour had been produced in the wine after treading, the fermenting must was run off into barrels called *toneles*, in which a quantity of spirit had been placed. This arrested the fermentation and the wine was then left to mature. This traditional method, although still used in some places, is becoming less common in the Douro, because workers tend to leave the countryside and migrate to the towns where they can get better wages. So modern methods have been introduced.

In these methods, a crusher–destalker is used, as in the making of beverage wines. Thence the crushed grapes are pumped into large vats or *cubas*. As it is important to extract the maximum colour from the fermenting must as quickly as possible, a technique of autovinification is used. Fig. 28 shows how this process works. The crushed grapes are pumped into the siphon vat up to a predetermined level. Once the fermentation starts, gas pressure forces the fermenting liquid in the sealed vat downwards, and up the side funnel shown in Fig. 28 into an open trough on the top of the tank. The wine comes out of the side funnel and fills the trough, showing how much colour has been extracted. This siphon autovinificator works rather like a cross between a coffee percolator and an automatic flush. There is a water valve, quite separate from the wine, which opens when the pressure reaches a certain level, and allows the wine to drain from the upper outside trough, back into the vat through the central tube. By its concentric arrangement, this tube forces the returning must to bounce off the inside roof of the vat and to spray down on to the cap of skins with considerable force, beating the colour out of the skins as it does so.

The siphon vat is an improvement on the *lagar*, which left the

Fig. 28

97

Autovinification

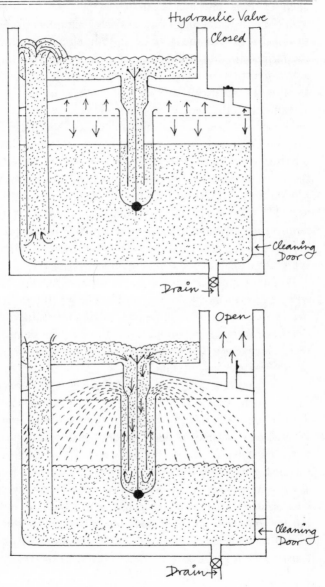

Hydraulic Valve

Closed

Cleaning Door

Drain

Open

Cleaning Door

Drain

whole fermenting mass open all the time, not only to the air but also to bacteria. However, it still leaves part of the must in the open for some time, and it still brings the skins into full contact with the fermenting must only at fairly long intervals. The ideal situation is to keep the skins in constant circulation throughout the fermenting must. This can be done by another method of autovinification, in which sealed vats of stainless steel are used. In these an electrically-driven shaft with vanes drives the cap of skins into the centre; attached to this central shaft is an Archimedean screw which forces the cap of skins down a central tube to the bottom, whence they emerge and again float to the top, thus ensuring that the skins are continually in contact with the fermenting must. By this method, the required colour is produced more quickly and without risk of contamination. The vats are thermostatically controlled to ferment at the best temperature. Although temperature control is also possible in the siphon vat, the wine, being open at the top to the air, is subject to oxidation and contamination by bacteria.

Whatever method is used, frequent tests are taken in a small white porcelain bowl, looking rather like an American sailor's hat, so that when the right amount of colour is achieved, which should be with the maximum sugar, the wine can be run off into the maturing vats or *toneles*, into which spirit has been placed to stop further fermentation.

The wine, muted by the spirit, is allowed to remain in the *quintas* in the Upper Douro region until the spring. In the old days, the wine had to wait until the Spanish snows melted and the River Douro started to flood, as only then was it possible to move the wine in boats, the ancient Barcos Rabellos, which travelled down-river to Porto. It was a very treacherous journey, as there were many rapids. This journey is nowadays impossible, because dams have been constructed across the river for power; but for some time the wine has been moved in casks or tanker, by rail or road, down to the shippers' lodges at Vila Nova de Gaia, where it is checked by the inspectors of the Instituto.

There are as many different styles of port as there are of sherry. Fig. 29, page 100, summarizes their maturation. Some styles of port are 'Vintage', that is to say they are all wines of one year. Others, shown by shaded casks, are blends of several years. Yet there is only one Vintage port and the rules controlling its production are very strict. It must be bottled between the second and third year after harvest. Ports, being red wines, throw a considerable sediment and young port bottled for Vintage will throw this in the bottle. Such ports must therefore mature on their lees. The lees are heavy and the wine thus needs to be very carefully decanted from the bottle before serving.

The second column of Fig. 29, Late-Bottled Vintage, deals with wine that has been kept a little longer in cask, with production strictly controlled. It must be bottled between the fourth and the sixth year after the harvest. Some of the sediment will have been thrown in the cask before the fourth year. Much more is thrown in the fifth year, so that a port bottled as a Late-Bottled Vintage in its fourth year will be suitable for laying down and will mature slowly. Although throwing much less in bottle than Vintage, it will require decanting in the same way as a Vintage port. This system is particularly suitable for ports which, though not from the finest years, can be softened a little by accelerated ageing in cask.

However, a Late-Bottled Vintage port which has been bottled during the fifth or sixth year will have thrown most of its deposit in the cask and is bottled ready for immediate drinking, as is indicated in Fig. 29 by the bottle standing beside a glass.

'Port with Date of Harvest' is another category allowed by the Portuguese authorities. This may not be bottled before the eighth year. The date of vintage may be stated on the label but it is not Vintage port even though it is from a single year.

These three wines are all ports of a single year; nevertheless there is a fourth 'dated port' known as 'Port of Indicated Age'. This is a blend of wine of different ages, adjudged by experts to be similar in character to wines of a single vintage matured in

Maturation of Ports

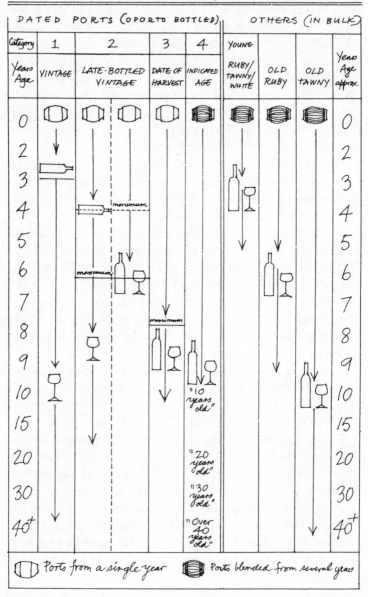

	DATED PORTS (OPORTO BOTTLED)				OTHERS (IN BULK)			
Category	1	2	3	4	YOUNG			Years Age approx.
Years Age	VINTAGE	LATE-BOTTLED VINTAGE	DATE OF HARVEST	INDICATED AGE	RUBY/ TAWNY/ WHITE	OLD RUBY	OLD TAWNY	

Ports from a single year   Ports blended from several years

cask. The only ages which may be indicated on the label are ten, twenty, thirty or over forty years old. They are in fact fine old Tawny ports, tawny in colour through ageing in the wood. Oxidation dulls the bright red or purple of the original wine, which pales as the years go on. Oxidation also changes the fruitiness of the original wine to a more nutty flavour. Thus two port wines, both 25 years old, one a Vintage and one a Tawny, could readily be distinguished by eye and 'on the nose'. To the eye the Vintage would look a garnet colour and the Tawny would look a lovely light tawny brown. The Vintage would smell fruity and the Tawny would smell nutty. Each is beautiful port, for its own occasion.

All four wines so far described must be bottled in Oporto, or more correctly in Vila Nova de Gaia. They must, in short, be Portuguese bottled. On the right hand side of Fig. 29 are the commercial ports, all blended, which may be bottled in the United Kingdom. Ruby is a port which has been aged in wood for about three to five years and is blended from wines of two or three years. White port has been made from white grapes in exactly the same manner as that made from red grapes – fermented on the skins, but golden in colour. Young Tawny is probably a commercial blend of Ruby and White ports. It will not have the quality of the older Tawnies, but will find a ready market because of its reasonable price.

A shipper in this country might, for economic or other reasons, get a good young Ruby blended from three fairly good years, bottle it and lay it down. After a few years, when it has thrown a crust, he could sell it as a Crusted port at a better price than he would otherwise obtain. If Late-Bottled Vintage port should become very expensive and the taste for Crusted port persists, this could be a very reasonable commercial alternative.

Next comes Old Ruby. These ports have been blended and matured for a minimum of seven years, going up to about ten years, after which they will become fine old Tawny ports, as shown in the last column: again these are blended ports, bottled

in the United Kingdom. They cannot be called 'Ports of Indicated Age' like '20 year-old Tawny', because they have been
bottled in the United Kingdom and not in Portugal.

Other fortified wines

There are other fortified wines besides sherry and port, and
they too have their individual methods of production. The most
important of them is Madeira, taking its name from the Portuguese island where it is made, some seven hundred miles out
in the Atlantic from Lisbon.

Though Madeira is a very small island, some of its mountains
are about 6000 feet high, considerably higher than any in the
British Isles. Only the coastal belt is cultivated and that is very
steep indeed. The vineyards are perched on terraces, ranged up
the cliffs from the sea. The island was discovered in 1410 when a
Portuguese captain named Gonçalvez, known as Zarco (cross-
eyed), landed in the Bay of Funchal and decided to settle his
people there. The island was heavily wooded, so he started a fire
to make a small clearing. The fire raged for seven years and all
the trees on the island were burned. Now the island rises gaunt
out of the sea. Its volcanic rock is of great value in that water
accumulates in its crevices, but nevertheless drains well; and
of course the trees burning for seven years made a great deal of
potash, a very good fertilizer, thus creating ideal conditions for
the vine.

The vine is not the only crop grown on this island. Next in
size to the vine crop comes sugar-cane and then bananas. Cultivation of the vine in Madeira is hard work. Everything has to be
carried up or down the precipitous paths by hand. This applies
to fertilizers as well as to the grapes themselves, or their juice at
harvest time. The vines are trained mostly in two ways: either
on high wires as in Alsace, or on the traditional trellises where the
grapes hang down from the top. This island is at the equatorial
side of the northern vineyard band, and therefore the sun is
hot. Keeping the grapes away from the soil ensures that they do

not get too much heat, which would burn the leaves and prevent the grapes from ripening properly.

Four vine varieties are grown on the island, and all four, the Sercial, the Malmsey, the Verdelho and the Bual give their names to styles of Madeira wine. Sercial takes its name from the village of Seixal on the northern side of the island, whereas Malmsey is a corruption of Malvasia, the vine imported from Cyprus. The Sercial vine is said to be a relation of the Riesling.

Some Madeiras are made by the port method (stopping fermentation with spirit before it is complete), but some are fortified after fermentation is complete, as in the case of sherry. The *solera* system of blending may be used for either. Another peculiarity is the use of cane spirit, because local sugar-cane is plentiful and therefore cane spirit is cheap and easily obtainable.

The unique factor which singles out Madeira from all other wines, fortified or otherwise, is the process of *estufado*. This is literally cooking the wine. In the eighteenth and nineteenth centuries, there was an active shipping trade between Europe (and England in particular) and South America, Australia and South Africa. The ships sailed out with the merchandise needed in those distant markets and returned with skins, wool and grain. Before the ships sailed through the tropics, however, their captains were careful to top up their water tanks, and Madeira was well-known for its water supply. Having, on the outward journey, a certain amount of space, and being businessmen, the captains took on Madeira wine to sell at their destination, or failing that to bring back to England. In due course the ships reached the area of light winds close to the equator, known as the doldrums, where ships under sail were often becalmed for weeks at a time. The wine in the hold would gradually get hot, and would reach a temperature over 38°C (100°F). Then over the rest of the voyage, it would cool down again. It would also be jolted about, and it may seem surprising that when the wine was broached in Australia, it was still good, and even better than when it was shipped, for it had taken on a special flavour.

Scientists who have looked at this phenomenon in the present century concluded that the gradual heating and cooling of the wine not only gave Madeira its special flavour, but rendered it proof against practically every malady that can affect wine. A glass of Madeira can be left open to the air for a long time without losing its flavour. This cannot be said of any other wine.

Of course the people of Madeira were not slow to appreciate this great bonus, and so they made their wine in such a way as to imitate the conditions in the sailing ships. The *estufa* system came into being. The wine, having been made and racked, is placed in large tanks which are heated to a temperature of 50°C (122°F) and kept at that temperature for not less than 90 days. Seals are placed on the taps to ensure that no wine is added or removed, and the recording thermometer is also sealed to ensure that the temperature is maintained for the required time.

Sercial, the driest Madeira, was popular in this country at the end of the last century, as 'elevenses'. In Victorian times a visit to the family solicitor or bank manager would often end with a glass of Madeira, usually with a slice of plain cake (later to be called Madeira cake). Verdelho is not so well-known in this country, but has a pleasant fruitiness which may come from employing the port method of fortification. Bual and Malmsey are very popular as after-dinner drinks, which many prefer to port. Madeira is also extremely useful in the kitchen and can be used to add flavour to sauces and soups. Stewed kidneys and oxtail, particularly, will be heartened by a spoonful of Malmsey.

Another fortified wine having great value in the kitchen is Marsala. It comes from Marsala, at the tip of Sicily, off the toe of Italy. The wine is used for the famous sweet dish Zabaglione and for Escalope de Veau Marsala. But strangely, this may be said to be a truly British wine. Two British merchants, Mr. Smith and Mr. Woodhouse, who visited Marsala towards the end of the eighteenth century, were responsible for its development. They thought that the wine had great possibilities, but could not be traded in its natural form. They fortified it and added sweetening. This they obtained by boiling down pure grape must, which they called *vino cotto*, 'cooked wine', not to be confused with the cooked wine from Madeira. This blend became very popular, and when in 1800 Nelson visited the island, he tasted the wine of Marsala, found it good and placed an order for the fleet. Fig. 30 shows Nelson's instructions added in his own handwriting; he had recently lost his right arm and was learning to write with his left hand.

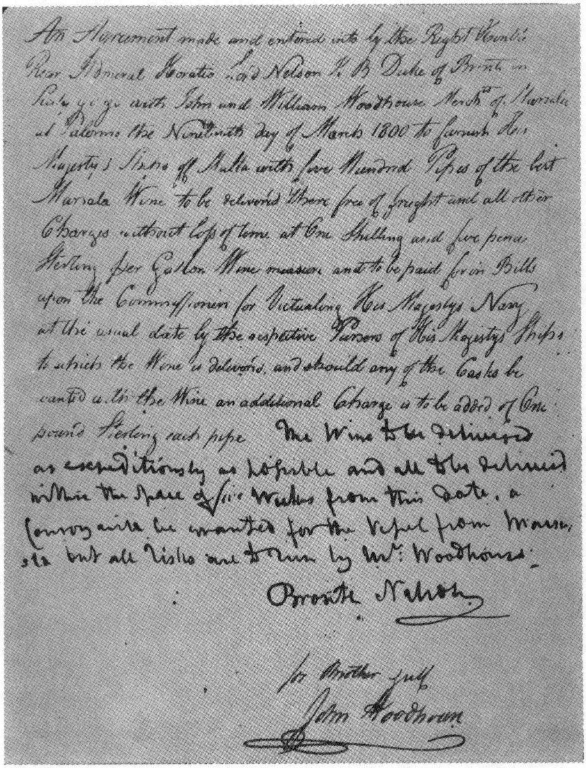
An Agreement made and entered into by the Right Honble
Rear Admiral Horatio Lord Nelson K. B Duke of Bronte in
Sicily &c &c with John and William Woodhouse Merchts of Marsala
at Palermo the Nineteenth day of March 1800 to furnish His
Majesty's Ships off Malta with five Hundred Pipes of the best
Marsala Wine to be delivered there free of freight and all other
Charges without loss of time at One Shilling and five pence
Sterling per Gallon Wine measure and to be paid for in Bills
upon the Commissioners for Victualing His Majesty's Navy
at the usual date by the respective Pursers of His Majesty's Ships
to which the Wine is delivered, and should any of the Casks be
wanted with the Wine an additional Charge is to be added of One
pound Sterling each pipe The Wine to be delivered
as expeditiously as possible and all to be delivered
within the Space of five Weeks from this date. a
Convoy will be wanted for the Vessel from Marsa-
-la but all Risks are to run by Mr. Woodhouse.

Bronte Nelson

for Brother self
John Woodhouse

Fig. 30

Other fortified wines include Malaga from the south of Spain, formerly known under the name of 'Mountain', which may yet become fashionable again; and the strong, sweet wine of Tarragona from the northeast corner of Spain, so popular in Lancashire. In France there are fortified wines called *vins doux naturels*, natural sweet wines. These are well-named, their sweetness coming from the original grape, preserved by the addition of alcohol before fermentation is complete – much as in the case of port. The Muscatel grape is the one most often used.

Vermouths are fortified wines which have been flavoured, and they come mainly from the south of France and the north of Italy. Both countries now produce a range of dry white, sweet white and sweet red Vermouths. Originally the French Vermouth was all sweet. The apparently paradoxical 'dry Martini' cocktail, first made with French Vermouth, was in fact named after the barman who invented it.

The name Vermouth derives from the German *vermut*, meaning the herb wormwood (*artimesia absinthia*). This herb is very bitter, yet has certain curative and exhilarating properties. Vermouths are flavoured not only with wormwood but also with many other herbs and alpine plants. They make an appetizing addition to cocktails and are most useful in the kitchen.

Many countries, including Britain, make Vermouths and other fortified wines. Where claims of special tonic, restorative and curative properties are made for them, these are required to be substantiated on the label by the laws of most countries.

Fortified wines fill a very important need in the wine-drinking habits of the world. They are more likely to be used before and after meals, than with them.

Spirit manufacture

Many references to spirits have already been made, as for example when explaining how fortified wines are prepared. But when it comes to defining what a spirit is, either in legal or scientific terms, there are difficulties. The Customs and Excise Act of 1952 says that spirits means spirits of any description, including liquors mixed with spirits, and mixtures, compounds or preparations made with spirits, but excepting methylated spirits. This definition is not, however, very enlightening. Add to this the fact that spirits can be made in any part of the world and from practically any fermentable base, and definition may seem even further away. Indeed, little help comes from the fact that the process of distillation, carried on long enough, will produce a completely colourless, odourless, tasteless liquid – distinguishable only as pure ethyl alcohol – whatever base material was used to start the process. But, *for the purposes of the spirits trade*, the fermentable base materials of spirits, other than fruit spirits and rum, are restricted to grape and grain; and from there a definition starts to formulate. To the trade, a spirit is a liquid of high alcoholic content which is obtained by distillation from such fermentable materials. It must be distilled only to a point where it is purified, yet still retains sufficient by-products to impart the particular characteristics of the original base material. It is only necessary to add that distillation means the separation of alcohol from other substances in a liquid, by the application of heat.

Wines are of fairly low alcoholic strength: about 10° Gay-Lussac (GL). Fortified wines are stronger: about 20°GL, and they can only be made at that strength because they have been fortified with spirits. Fig. 31 shows the various strengths of wines, fortified wines, and spirits, and also gives a comparison

Fig. 31 (2°US proof = 1°GL)

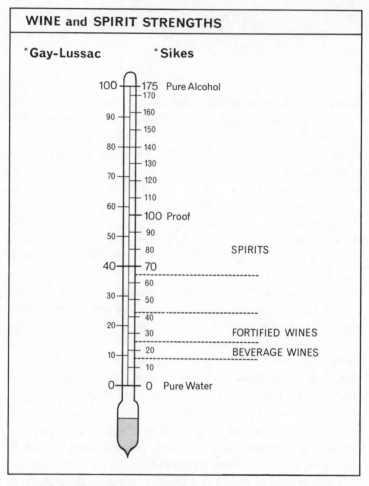

WINE and SPIRIT STRENGTHS

°Gay-Lussac   °Sikes

100 — 175 Pure Alcohol
         170
90 — 160
     150
80 — 140
     130
70 — 120
     110
60 — 100 Proof
50 — 90
     80   SPIRITS
40 — 70
     60 - - - - - - - - - - - - - -
30 — 50
     40 - - - - - - - - - - - - - -
20 — 30   FORTIFIED WINES
     20   BEVERAGE WINES
10 — - - - - - - - - - - - - - - - -
     10
0 — 0   Pure Water

between the Gay-Lussac scale used on the continent of Europe, Sikes scale used in the UK, and the proof scale used in the USA. You will see that the conversion is 40:70:80 (GL:UK:USA). A mark has been made on the figure at 42°Sikes, because that is the strength at which British Customs start taxing spirits as such – so much tax per degree Sikes. The normal strength at which spirits are sold in the UK is 70°Sikes.

How can such strengths be attained, when the normal maximum strength obtained by fermentation is only 18°GL (33° Sikes)? Wine may be considered as a comparatively weak mixture of alcohol and water, with some flavouring elements. To get a higher degree of concentration of the alcohol, these two liquids must be separated; but, unlike a mixture of oil and water, where the oil floats on top of the water and can easily be separated by running off, the alcohol-water mixture is completely integrated. The molecules of each substance stick together closely at all levels of the mixture, much as burrs collected on a country walk attach themselves to the clothes.

However, alcohol and water, although both colourless and odourless liquids, have different physical characteristics, one being that they have different volatilities. Water freezes at 0°C (32°F) and boils at 100°C (212°F), whereas ethyl alcohol freezes at −133°C (−207°F) and boils at 78°C (172°F). So there are apparently two ways in which they could be separated, by cooling to below 0°C (32°F), or heating to above 78°C (172°F). The former method, called 'congelation', is sometimes used in Canadian homes to make 'applejack'. Cider is put out to freeze on a winter night. In the morning the ice which has formed is thrown away, and the remaining liquid is put out again the next night; after three or four nights the strength of the residue has increased somewhat. This method is illegal, not because it evades duty, but because it has great dangers, in retaining all the poisonous higher alcohols (fusel-oils). This part of the mixture must be got rid of; although it was present in the original cider or wine, it was then diluted to a safe degree.

Distillation

Congelation being dangerous – and rather ineffective, as the molecules tend to stick more closely together under cold conditions – distillation must be the answer. Distillation is separation by vaporization, not by boiling. Merely raising the temperature of a 'wash' to 78°C (172°F) will not vaporize all the alcohol and leave all the water in a liquid state, because water will vaporize at any temperature, even as ice. Our lungs depend on water vapour to keep them lubricated. By the slow heating of the alcoholic wash, a mixture of alcohol and water in liquid form is changed into a similar mixture in vapour form; but, when the liquid has held a temperature of 78°C (172°F) for some time and the temperature then starts to rise again, *all* the alcohol will have changed to the vapour state, but only part of the water and less volatile fusel-oils will have done so.

Fig. 32 shows the principles of distillation. A boiler, containing the alcoholic wash, is heated by the fire beneath; the boiler leads into a pipe at the top, retaining the vapour. At the further end of the pipe, the vapour is condensed by a cooling bath, in which the pipe is coiled like a worm. This method, with refinements which will be explained, is known as the 'pot still' method.

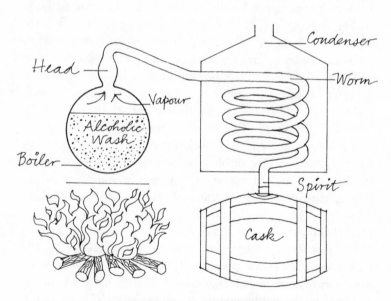

Fig. 32   *Principles of Distillation*

Several spirits are produced by this particular method of distillation: Cognac brandy, Scotch malt whisky, Irish whiskey, Bourbon whiskey, rum and some other spirits. The details of the still vary slightly, but the manner of carrying out the distillation is the same. The distillation is usually done in two stages, but sometimes, and for some spirits, it is done in three or even four stages. In the first stage, the wash is heated until all the alcohol has vaporized, and all the vapour is condensed in the worm and collected in a receiving vessel. The liquid thus collected amounts to about one third of the original volume of wash. After the boiler has been emptied out and refilled, the process is repeated with a new charge of wash, twice, after which enough distillate has been collected to fill the boiler.

This *brouillis*, as it is called in Cognac, or 'low wines', as it is called in Scotland, which has a strength of about 35°GL, is then redistilled. The first vapours coming off contain a high proportion of volatile poisons, particularly acetaldehyde, which has a boiling-point of 28°C (82°F). Passing from the domed head at the top of the boiler, they condense in the worm and are collected in a special receiver. Some of the less-volatile substances fall back into the boiler, to be revaporized: the molecules of the different substances shake loose from each other. The volatile poisons are lighter than alcohol, having a lower specific gravity, and can be detected by using a hydrometer. When the hydrometer readings, and the stillman's nose, indicate that purer alcohol is coming over, the stillman will switch the stream of water-white liquid coming from the worm into another receiver. As the distillation progresses, a rank smell and a rising hydrometer reading will indicate that the poisonous fusel-oils are starting to come over in greater concentration; so the stillman again switches the stream back to the first receiver. He has, during this second distillation, separated the poisonous 'heads' and 'tails', called respectively 'foreshots' and 'feints' in Scotland, from the good 'heart'. .

It can be seen that this method is laborious, requiring the still to be emptied and refilled four times; and that the separation is somewhat arbitrary, leaving some of the volatile and non-volatile poisons in the 'heart', and some of the alcohol in the heads and tails. The alcohol in the heads and tails can be extracted by putting them back for redistillation with the next batch of *brouillis* or low wines. The poisons can be extracted from the hearts by further redistillation, as in Irish whiskey, or by long maturation in wood as with Cognac brandy and Scotch malt whisky.

The spirit which goes into the casks is water-white in colour, and has a strength of about 70°GL; after the normal maturation period of three years, its fieriness has abated, it has taken on a golden colour, and its aroma is pleasant and gentle. During this time, the various constituents of the spirit have reacted with each other, producing compounds to build up the flavour and aroma; there has also been a gradual evaporation of the liquids through the pores of the wood. The wood, in turn, has added tannin and colour; as much as three pounds in weight of oak products may be assimilated by the spirit in a new cask of Cognac brandy in one year. The microclimate of the maturing sheds or cellars will also determine the character of the spirit. Spirit matured in a warm, dry, atmosphere will lose bulk but keep its strength; while spirit matured in a colder, damper, climate – as in England – will lose strength but keep its bulk. Whichever condition applies, a large amount of alcohol will escape into the atmosphere. In Scotland, as much alcohol escapes as is drunk in the whole United Kingdom; in Cognac, as much as is consumed in the whole of France – there they call it 'the angels' share'.

The pot still, with its slow and laborious filling and emptying of the boiler, remained the only method of distillation until 1830, when an Irish customs officer named Aeneas Coffey invented a patent still. His design is still in use today, and is illustrated in Fig. 33. Basically, the apparatus consists of two tall columns, each about sixty feet in height, called the 'analyser' and the 'rectifier'. The wash is broken down into its constituent

Fig. 33

113

Coffey Still

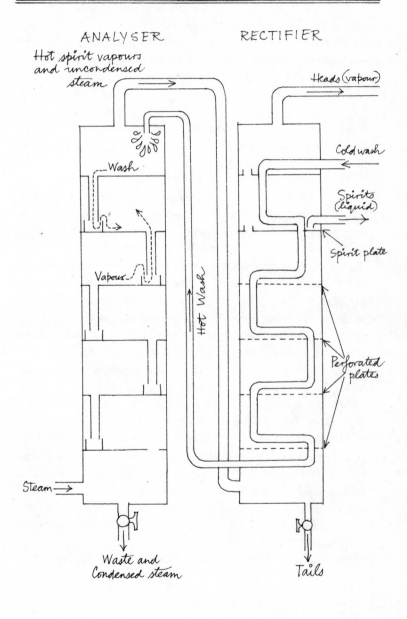

ANALYSER

RECTIFIER

Hot spirit vapours
and uncondensed
steam

Heads (vapour)

Cold wash

Spirits
(liquid)

Wash

Spirit plate

Vapour

Hot Wash

Perforated
plates

Steam

Waste and
Condensed steam

Tails

vapours, or analysed, in the analyser, and the vapours are selec-
tively condensed or rectified, in the rectifier.

Wash which has been heated in the rectifier is pumped into the
top of the analyser, and trickles down the column through a
tortuous passage of plates and bubble caps; steam is injected into
the bottom of the column, and rises, bubbling through the wash
as it goes. In so doing, it heats the wash above the boiling point
of alcohol, and cools itself in the same process by heat exchange.
The condensed steam, together with the unvaporized part of the
wash, runs down to the bottom of the column and out; this
liquid is equivalent to the spent wash left in the boiler of the pot
still at the end of the first distillation.

The vapours rise, and pass out of the analyser through a pipe
at the top, whence they are led to enter the bottom of the rectifier.
The rectifier has cooling pipes running down through it; these
are the pipes into which cold wash is pumped at the top. Again
by heat exchange, the wash is heated by the hot vapours, and
the hot vapours are cooled by the cold wash, the net result being
that the rectifier is hot at the bottom and cold at the top. As the
vapours rise, therefore, they cool, and fairly near the bottom
of the rectifier the less volatile fusel-oils condense; a wire grid
is stretched across the column to help them do so, much as dew
will condense on the gossamer webs of lawn-spiders in autumn.
Being condensed, the liquid falls to the bottom of the rectifier,
where it is heated and revaporized: it then rises again, and is
condensed again, and so on, with each revaporization shaking
loose more individual molecules from each other.

This process continues all the way up the column, the temperature steadily falling until a point is reached where the
temperature is about 78°C (172°F). At this point, instead of a
grid, a solid plate is stretched across the column, in order to
collect the condensing vapours which will by this time be fairly
pure alcohol. At a slightly higher level, another plate is placed
to prevent the more volatile impurities from condensing and
falling back to contaminate the alcohol. Most of the heads pass

out of the top of the rectifier and are condensed in a worm; the less volatile impurities eventually fall to the bottom of the rectifier and are collected with the heads. In case there are any remaining traces of alcohol in them, they are fed back into the wash pipe to go through the still again.

As long as cold wash is pumped into the top of the rectifier, and at the same time steam is pumped into the bottom of the analyser, the still will continue to operate; for this reason, it is often called the continuous still. There are many other designs of continuous still, but the Coffey still illustrated reveals the basic principles of all of them.

The spirit coming from a patent or continuous still is not completely pure. It still contains sufficient impurities to require a period of maturation. But the spirit is not nearly so pungent as that from a pot still, because it contains less of the 'congeners', as the impurities are sometimes called. It is therefore possible to tell the difference between a pot-still and a patent-still spirit on the nose, by the pungency of the former.

Types of spirit

Having established the two methods of distillation, the next step is to consider the various types of spirit and what they are made from. In general terms, alcohol can be produced from the fermentation of any sugar; so wash, and therefore spirit, can be produced from any sugar solution, or from honey, or from the natural sugar of fruit. Table 2 shows some of the various spirits and their origins. Brandy is made from grapes, but brandy is by no means the only fruit spirit. Plums, apples, pears, cherries, strawberries and raspberries all contain natural sugar which can be fermented to give an alcoholic product for distillation. Sugar-cane also contains fermentable sugar, used to make rum. But there is another category of carbohydrates contained in some of the other spirits shown – starch. Starch is a very large, tough molecule, containing 48 atoms, and the ordinary enzymes of yeast are unable to work on it. However, there are enzymes

SPIRIT ORIGINS		
Pip fruits	GRAPES	COGNAC, ARMAGNAC, Brandies
	APPLES, PEARS	CALVADOS, Poire
Stone fruits	CHERRIES	Kirsch
	PLUMS	Slivovitz, Mirabelle, etc.
Soft fruits		Framboise, Fraise, etc.
Grains		WHISKY–EY, Gin*, Vodka
Other Vegetable	SUGAR CANE	RUM, Gin*, Vodka
	SUGAR BEET	Vodka*
	DATES	Arrack
	POTATO	Vodka*, Schnapps*
	CACTUS	Tequila
	and many others	

*Flavoured spirits

which will turn it into fermentable sugar, and these occur in any living plant which itself needs sugar to feed on.

If barley is steeped in water for a period and then exposed to gentle warmth, this simulates the action of rain and sun, and the barley will start to sprout. At this time the germ of the grain gives forth an enzyme called diastase, which turns the starch of the grain into a sugar called maltose; this sugar can be fermented by yeast to produce an alcoholic wash. This is the basis of malt whisky. (This enzyme, diastase, is so powerful that it will also convert the starch of unmalted grains, such as wheat, rye or maize, to maltose, when mashed together with their ground or cooked grains and hot water.) The growth of the barley, as it converts its starch to sugar, must be stopped, lest the barley sprout should feed on the sugar as it would in nature, and consume it. It is stopped by heating in a kiln. In the case of malt whisky, the fire that heats the kiln is of peat.

Malt whisky is, because of the peat smoke, and because of its distillation by the pot still method, a very pungent spirit. Different areas of Scotland give different aromas and degrees of pungency to the final blend of 'Scotch'. The Lowlands produce a malt whisky that is soft and subtly flavoured, while the Highlands, particularly in the valley of the River Spey, produce a whisky redolent of peat and heather. The water of this district, running off granite and filtered through peat, has much to do with this. The Western Isles, especially Islay, produce the most pungent whiskies of all; and it is not too fanciful to imagine that the sea-wrack can be tasted in them.

These whiskies were originally too pungent to appeal to any but the hardy Scots, and until the arrival of the Coffey still were little sold outside Scotland; but when the pungency of the malt whiskies was softened by grain whisky produced in the Coffey still, a Scotch was born that would captivate the world. The grains used in grain whisky are maize (which has to be ground and pressure-cooked before it is amenable), unmalted barley and malted barley, which alone provides the diastase necessary to turn the whole starchy mass into maltose.

Scotch whiskies are blended, after their compulsory three-year maturation period, to suit the market. Certain countries will swear by one brand, others by another. Diligent market research has determined the choice of blend. A blend may consist of as many as fifty different malt whiskies, amounting to perhaps 35% of the bulk, the remainder being grain whisky from a single distillery. There are about one hundred and ten malt distilleries in Scotland, and ten grain distilleries producing much more spirit. The grain distilleries also export spirit from Scotland, after redistillation, for making into gin and vodka; but spirit for Scotch Whisky must be produced and matured in Scotland, and nowhere else.

Brandy can be, and is, produced wherever wine is produced from grapes; but two brandies stand out for their quality, and for the fact that their production is strictly controlled by law –

Fig. 34

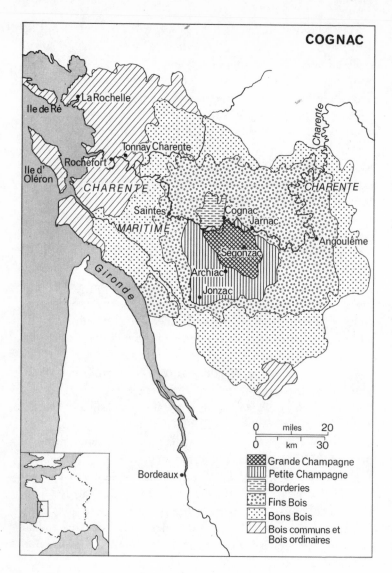

in each case French law, for the brandies are Cognac and Armagnac. The Cognac region lies on the Atlantic coast of France, just north of Bordeaux, and consists of a central chalky district surrounded concentrically by districts of coarser soils. The grape of this region, the Ugni Blanc, locally known as the St. Emilion, produces a thin, acid wine; but from this wine can be distilled the finest spirit in the whole world. The method used is the pot still, and the shape of the still and its size are laid down by law. The spirit must mature in the region for not less than one year, and the finest spirits are matured for three or four.

The finest brandies come from the three innermost districts, Grande Champagne, Petite Champagne and Borderies, each of which has its own *Appellation*; a further *Appellation*, that of Fine Champagne, signifies a Cognac blended only from Grande Champagne and Petite Champagne, with not less than 50% of Grande Champagne in the blend. The *Appellation* Cognac may be embellished by other marks: *** is commonly used to denote the export blend, which is usually about five years old, taking the average of the ages of the brandies in the blend. VSOP is another mark which is often seen, denoting a brandy of superior quality; this must be more than four years old, and is likely to be about seven years old. The initials stand for 'Very Special Old Pale', a distinction from the days in the last century when 'Brown Brandy' was the popular drink.

The next most famous spirit of France is Armagnac, a brandy distilled in the *Département* of Gers, south of Bordeaux in the foothills of the Pyrénées – the land of d'Artagnan and the Three Musketeers. Here, not only the Ugni Blanc, but also the Picpoul and even a hybrid grape variety are grown, and their wine is distilled in the special Armagnac still; this still is something between the pot still and the continuous still in design. In it, the wine is processed only once and produces spirit at no greater strength than 58° to 63°GL, compared with the 70°GL of Cognac. The differences between the two brandies do not stop here: Cognac brandy must be matured in casks made from oaks of the forests of Limousin and the Tronçais (east of Cognac), while Armagnac brandy is matured in the sappier, black oakwood of the Pyrénées. The spirits themselves differ, and each has its devotees.

Applejack has been mentioned as being distilled from cider; such a spirit is made in the Calvados region of France under strictly controlled conditions. This region lies along the coast of Normandy from Cherbourg to Dieppe, and for 30 to 50 miles inland; within it there are districts, ranging from the Pays d'Auge where the finest apple brandies are made in Cognac stills, through lesser districts where the Armagnac still may be used, to the ordinary 'cider spirit' made in continuous stills. All are good. It is perhaps strange that in England, a land famed for its cider, nothing is heard of an apple brandy being made; the answer may be related to the fact that the best brandies, like Cognac, are made from wines that are thin and poor – Normandy cider, green as grass, certainly fits this description.

This chapter would not be complete if it did not deal with the universal spirit, variously known as *marc* (properly *eau-de-vie-de-marc*), *grappa*, *bagaçeira*, and other names applicable to every other country where wine is produced. The mass of dry skins, pips and stalks left over after the last drop of must or wine has been extracted, still contains sugar which can be fermented to make a rough alcoholic wash, which in turn can be distilled to produce spirit. These spirits can vary considerably in quality, the best being the *marcs* of Champagne and of Burgundy; there are other good ones, but they need knowing. The poorer ones can, if taken often, damage the liver, and it is alleged that the Frenchman does not swear 'Ma foi' (meaning 'my faith!'), so much as 'Ma foie' (meaning 'my liver!').

Spirits from the grape and the apple have been mentioned, but there are many other fruits containing fermentable sugars, and hence there are many other 'fruit spirits'. Pears give Poire William; plums, Slivovitz, Quetsch or Mirabelle; cherries, Kirsch; raspberries, Framboise or Himbeergeist; strawberries,

Fraise; and, no doubt, there are spirits made from blackberries, loganberries, and cloudberries which certainly give their flavour to liqueurs.

Grain spirits, in the form of Scotch whisky, have also been considered; but the chart also shows whiskey (note the difference in spelling: only the Scotch variety is spelled *whisky* or *whiskies*; all the others are *whiskeys*). Bourbon, traditionally coming from Bourbon County in Kentucky, is made from a sour mash of grains, and contains not less than 51% of maize, with added rye and with malted barley to give the diastase. Irish whiskey is made from malt, with unmalted rye and wheat; Canadian rye whiskey is made from maize, rye and malted barley. Of the various types of whiskey, Straight Bourbon and Irish whiskey are made by the pot still method, and both have the typical pungency of this method of distillation. Canadian whiskey, however, is made in a patent still, and consequently has lighter characteristics.

Rum is a spirit made by distilling fermented sugar-cane products, usually molasses. It can be light- or full-flavoured, according to the distillation method, and light or dark in colour, depending on the amount of caramel added. It is usually manufactured in sugar-cane producing countries, but matured in more temperate climates. Under present British law, the minimum period of maturation is two years. There are many sugar-cane-producing countries in the world, but the word rum immediately turns the mind to the West Indies: to Jamaica, where the rum is full-flavoured and pungent, although light in colour, indicating that a pot still has been used. There are also Trinidad rums, Barbados rums, and the French rums of Martinique. As Martinique is part of metropolitan France, its rums count as produce of the EEC, with tariff advantages. Nearby, in Guyana, Demerara sugar, and hence Demerara rum, a blend of patent and pot-still rum, is produced.

Several of the spirits shown in Table 2 are marked thus*, denoting that they are flavoured. Grains do not provide the only starch that can be turned into sugar and fermented, although they provide the best; root vegetables such as potatoes and sugar-beet (which provides sugar direct) can be used as bases for spirits. Nevertheless, these root vegetables always give a rank flavour to the spirit, and this must be disguised. Many years ago, the Dutch found that they could distil a spirit from rye, but in those days they lacked the means of purifying it sufficiently to be palatable; they therefore flavoured it with juniper berries, which they called *genever*, or gin for short. The quality of the spirit has improved, but the flavour remains, though many further additives such as coriander, orris root, angelica root, liquorice and cardamom are now added to particular brands.

Several spirits are derived from root vegetables. The Schnapps, or Snaps, so beloved by Scandinavians, is produced from potatoes, and flavoured with caraway seed, or cumin. Vodka, which in Russian means 'little water', was traditionally made in the Baltic states from whatever crop happened to be surplus and, depending on the crop, was appropriately flavoured. Nowadays in England most vodka is produced from triple-distilled spirit (made in a continuous still), which has been further purified by filtration through activated charcoal until it is completely odourless and tasteless. The spirit may be obtained from grain or from imported molasses. In the latter case the spirit is known as cane spirit.

Flavouring of spirits, even in the sixteenth century when the Dutch made their gin, was not a new art. The monks, who were the pharmacists of the Middle Ages, knew the ability of alcohol to dissolve the medicinal element of herbs, and used it to compound their remedies. They knew three maladies: being of poor appetite, being surfeited by food, and being unwell the next morning. And for these they produced three remedies: the *apéritif*, the *digestif* and the *correctif*. In present times the first has remained as a Vermouth or flavoured wine, the second as a spirit or flavoured liqueur, and the third as bitters, now mostly known by trade names.

Liqueurs and how they are made

Liqueurs, the sweet and sometimes brightly-coloured drinks that are produced at the end of many social occasions, were originally made in monasteries. The word itself derives from the Latin *liquefacere* – to make liquid or to dissolve. Not only should the essential elements of a liqueur be dissolved and intimately blended together, but, taken after meals, they should help to dissolve and blend the foods already eaten. One famous liqueur was first used to revive monks who had wilted at their work, and, before finally being commercialized, the same liqueur was used to protect peasants and fishermen from malaria. The fundamental idea that a liqueur was first and foremost a medicine has persisted, and as recently as 1847 François Vincent Raspail – the forerunner of Pasteur – invented a liqueur which, he claimed destroyed 'the parasites held to be the cause of most human sickness'.

Kümmel, which means literally 'caraway', is an excellent example of the adaptation of a known digestive to the liqueur medium. A child no more than a week old may be given gripe water to drink: this is made from caraway. The caraway seed is often used in cakes for children. And in central Europe caraway seeds were served in small dishes with the cheese course, so that the seeds could be taken in a small spoon and sprinkled on the cheese. Kümmel is a caraway liqueur, and the combination of caraway and alcohol is a fine aid to digestion.

A liqueur is nothing but a spirit which has been sweetened and flavoured: this is its essential definition. The strength – in alcoholic terms – varies considerably between different types and brands, and the spirit may be any spirit. Malt whisky is used as the base spirit of some Scottish liqueurs; brandy is often used in French liqueurs, and rum in West Indian liqueurs; but many European liqueurs are based on plain spirits from a number of source materials, such as potato, sugar-beet, grain or molasses.

The sweetening agent may be honey, or sugar in various other forms, but the individuality of each liqueur comes neither from the spirit nor from the sweetening agent, but from the selection of flavouring agents, of which there is an immense variety. One well-known liqueur has as many as 130 different peels, roots, herbs, spices and other constituents contributing to its flavour. It is still held that to be a genuine digestive liqueur, a purifying or curative ingredient, or a combination of several or many of them, must be incorporated. Perhaps this derives from the writings of Hippocrates, the 'Father of Medicine', who in or about 460 BC claimed that the ancients practised the distillation of aromatic plants for medicinal purposes.

Flavouring agents form the most individual group of ingredients in liqueurs, and impart an air of excitement and mystery attractive to the consumer. Some aromas are water-soluble, and some are oil- or spirit-soluble. Some are not harmed by heating, others are. The choice of flavouring agent therefore determines to a large extent the method of extraction of the aroma from the base material. The three important methods are cold maceration (over a long time), hot infusion (over a short time), and distillation to produce an 'elixir'.

Maceration consists of soaking the flavouring material in alcohol or water to extract the flavour. This process may take from 24 hours up to a year. It is the only method that can be used in the case of aromatic plants, where not only the full freshness and fragrance of the aroma, but also the retention of their natural colour, is desired, or where the flavour would be destroyed by heating.

Hot infusion, or percolation, is an intensive variation of the maceration process, involving the circulation of hot spirit through a filter of the pulverized flavouring agent. The spirit is cycled on a closed circuit to extract essential oils. The hot infusion method is only suitable for flavouring agents stable to heat, but is a much faster process than maceration.

The distillation method consists of passing alcohol vapour through a filter of pulverized flavouring materials, or of distilling a mixture of alcohol or water with the materials. This method is reasonably quick and safe for the treatment of quite delicate agents, as it is possible to lower the temperature of distillation under vacuum. The elimination of 'heads' and 'tails' during distillation calls for the usual constraints, as only the middle fraction or 'heart' has the purity and strength necessary for the product. The distillates are almost water-white, strong and dry, and it is necessary to add colouring and sweetening materials to balance the product as a saleable liqueur.

It is also possible to extract flavour from certain types of ingredient, as for example the peel of citrus fruits, by mechanical pressure. Other ingredients are suitable for treatment with non-volatile compounds, such as fats, which can hold a bouquet for later extraction by alcohol.

The choice of flavours and ingredients which produce the distinguishing features of the great liqueurs are secret, and in most cases the actual recipes have never been written, but have been handed down from generation to generation by word of mouth. Certain of the ingredients are known to be used in some cases, but the permutations are too great for analysis to reveal all the truth. These ingredients fall into four main categories which identify the liqueurs themselves. So there are fruit liqueurs, citrus liqueurs, herb liqueurs (subdivided into those with a predominant flavour of one herb and those characteristic of mixed herbs) and bean and kernel liqueurs.

Fruit liqueurs

It is a common mistake to confuse fruit liqueurs with fruit brandies, although they may be consumed on similar occasions and both are used in the preparation of sweet dishes. However, they are quite different. Liqueurs are made by adding flavouring and sweetening agents to spirit. A fruit brandy, however, is a spirit in which the sugar of a fruit has been used for the original fermentation to produce a wash which has then been distilled, and this is the definition of *eaux-de-vie*. Hence Calvados, Kirsch, Slivovitz and other fruit brandies have been mentioned in the chapter dealing with spirits. It does not matter that fruits used in the production of fruit liqueurs have a sugar content: they have spirit added. This may be done by a straightforward compounding of fruit and spirit, or it may be by maceration or distillation.

Cherry Brandy, Apricot Brandy and Peach Brandy are all sweet liqueurs. Although they are all called brandies, they are not *eaux-de-vie*: they are liqueurs, and are produced in a number of countries, including England. Other famous fruit liqueurs include Maraschino from Italy, made from sour maraschino cherries and their crushed kernels, sometimes with sugar and flower-blossom perfumes added; Crème de Cassis, from the Dijon area, made from blackcurrants and grape brandy; the American Southern Comfort, very widely appreciated in the USA, having peach and orange flavours added to a base of Bourbon whiskey; Crème de Banane, favoured in Australia, having a deep banana bouquet emerging from pure spirit; and Suomuurain, sometimes called Lakka, a bittersweet liqueur culled from cloudberries in Finland in clement years.

Citrus liqueurs
Some of the best-known liqueurs are among those made from citrus fruits, and the single word curaçao has a considerable significance. Originally orange curaçao meant a liqueur made with fruit from Curaçao in the West Indies. But the term has become generic, and now is used to describe a range of liqueurs in which the predominant flavour derives from the peel of the orange. Curaçaos are water-white liqueurs to which colouring is added, so that they may be found in several colours – orange, blue, and white. The highly rectified white 'triple-sec' curaçao has a

strength of 78° proof: Cointreau is among the more popular of these triple-sec curaçaos. Grand Marnier, another well-known curaçao, is made in the Bordeaux region from a Cognac spirit base. It is blended to sell as Cordon Rouge, the higher strength, and Cordon Jaune, the lower strength.

An interesting variation on the curaçaos is Van der Hum – a South African liqueur made from nartjies, a native orange variant, and other flavouring ingredients. It was produced first by Dutch settlers in imitation of their beloved curaçao, but for some reason – could it have been their love of the liqueur? – they forgot who discovered it, and hence its name Van der Hum, 'Mister What's-his-name'.

The Americans, with their eternal gift for epitome, christened one of their earliest liqueurs Forbidden Fruit, because it was good as nectar. Made from shaddock, a type of grapefruit grown in the USA, Forbidden Fruit has a bittersweet flavour of citrus, and is marketed in an elaborate orb-shaped bottle. Rock and Rye, another American liqueur, based on rye whiskey, and deriving its name from the original bottle which had crystallized rock candy on its sides, is also flavoured with citrus fruits.

Many other countries have their citrus liqueurs, and among those that have attracted an export market are Aurum, from Italy; Filfar, from Cyprus; Kitron, from Greece; Mersin, from Turkey; Sabra, from Israel and Bergamot and Citronen-eis Likör from Germany.

Herb liqueurs

Herb liqueurs have a particular attraction for the palate, because of their subtlety of flavour, which in some cases derives from a number of mixed herbs, and in others from only one. Two Scotch whisky liqueurs, one old and one not so old, have mixed herb flavouring. Drambuie, the oldest and best-known, can be quoted for its popularity and its history, but not for its herbal ingredients. The recipe was handed by Bonnie Prince Charlie to Mackinnon of Strathaird when Mackinnon gave shelter to the Prince after the unsuccessful rebellion of '45, and the Mackinnons produce and market Drambuie by a secret formula to this day. Glen Mist, the second-oldest whisky liqueur, though young by comparison with Drambuie, has had a chequered career. A substitute was made in Eire for nearly twenty years from 1945, when Scotch whisky and sugar were in short supply. It is flavoured with a blend of herbs, spices and honey, and is claimed to be the driest of Scotch whisky liqueurs. Benedictine is a name to conjure with among liqueurs. At the beginning of the sixteenth century, the monk Don Bernardo Vincelli invented the recipe at the Abbey in Fécamp. It revived the tired monks, and was successful in combating malaria in the surrounding countryside. King Francis I of France visited the Abbey in 1534 to investigate 'Benedictine ad majorem Dei gloriam'. The *Procureur Fiscal* of the Abbey saved the recipe when the Abbey was destroyed in the French Revolution. The recipe passed into the hands of a wine-merchant, Monsieur Alexandre le Grand, who developed Benedictine commercially, with a special label bearing the initials DOM, for Deo Optimo Maximo – 'To God, most good and great' – on every bottle.

Near Grenoble in the French Alps is Chartreuse, where the ancient Carthusian Order was founded by St. Bruno. Here in 1848, a group of army officers billeted at the monastery were offered a *digestif*. How long the monks had kept their secret is not known, but so intrigued were the officers that the fame of Chartreuse spread rapidly, and in 1860 a distillery was built at Fourvoirie to meet a rapidly growing commercial demand for the liqueur, which is marketed green at 96° proof and yellow at 75° proof.

Two other liqueurs from French monasteries are Trappistine and Vieille Cure. Trappistine, from the monks of the Abbey of Grace-Dieu, comes from the herbs of the Doubs Mountains. It is distilled with Armagnac, and is green-yellow in colour. Vieille Cure, from the Abbey of Canon in the Gironde, is made from 50 root and aromatic plants steeped in Armagnac and Cognac. The

Opposite: Cognac Pot Still

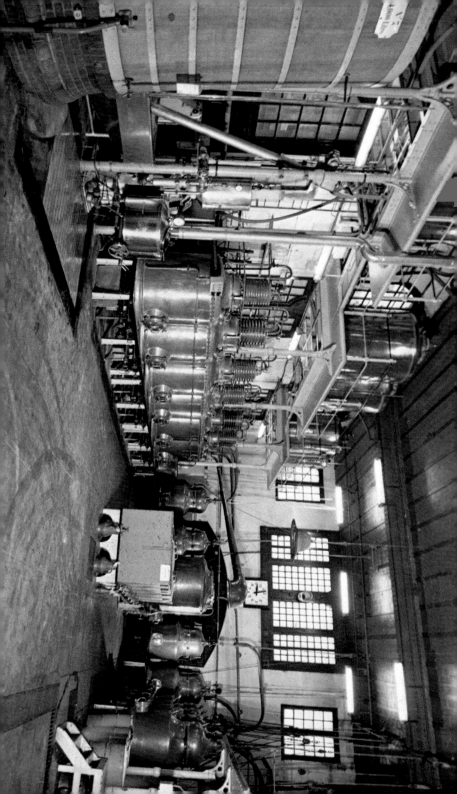

recipes are well-preserved secrets surviving from mediaeval times.

Every country which produces a spirit produces liqueurs, and there are thousands of them. It follows that Drambuie, Glen Mist, Benedictine, and Chartreuse are by no means the only liqueurs made from mixed herbs – there are hundreds of them, and generally their recipes are guarded. Liqueurs with the flavour of single herbs predominating can be described more subjectively however, and an excellent example is Absinthe. The original product marketed by Henri Louis Pernod was made from aromatic herbs from the Jura mountains, including aniseed, coriander, fennel, hyssop, liquorice and wormwood. It was of high alcoholic strength, and the proportion of wormwood was harmful; consequently it was banned by France and Switzerland before the Great War. A substitute, in which wormwood was eliminated, was marketed as Pernod, and this dry liqueur is still consumed in the same way as Absinthe – with water and ice, which turns it milky. Ladies of the Edwardian era found Absinthe so dry that it was taken through a lump of sugar, drop by drop, in a special spoon.

Pernod is perhaps the best-known of the aniseed liqueurs, but many others are produced, and Anisette, first made by Marie Brizard of Bordeaux in the eighteenth century, is an important example. With her nephew Jean-Baptiste Roger, she compounded Anisette and other liqueurs, and the firm of Brizard today is acknowledged as a founder of the French liqueur industry. Ouzo, another aniseed liqueur, is produced in Greece and Cyprus and is drunk 'on the rocks', when it turns slowly milky.

Caraway is undoubtedly the flavouring agent which, with aniseed and mint, predominates among the single-herb-flavoured liqueurs. The properties of caraway, already mentioned, have been known for centuries, and the Dutch cultivated the caraway plant extensively in the Middle Ages. Lucas Bols was the first to make Kümmel in Amsterdam in 1575, and Bolskümmel is famous still. The taste for Kümmel was carried east towards

Opposite: Still Room of the Benedictine Factory at Fécamp

Russia and the Baltic following a visit of Peter the Great of Russia to Amsterdam in 1696. The Riga Kümmels of the Wolf-schmidt family have subsequently found their way to a considerable market in England.

Danzig Goldwasser is an interesting liqueur made in Danzig by Der Lachs since 1598. The liqueur, water-white, is flavoured with aniseed and caraway, and gold flakes have been added from the days when it was believed that gold had properties for treating certain diseases. Since the destruction of Der Lachs' distilleries in Danzig during the World War, Danzig Goldwasser (and Danzig Silberwasser also, with silver flakes instead of gold) is produced in West Berlin.

Finally, among those single-flavoured, are the mint liqueurs, produced by practically every liqueur manufacturer. Mint in the form of *crème de menthe* is renowned as a *digestif*.

Bean and kernel liqueurs

Bean and kernel liqueurs, the final identifiable group among the digestive spirits, are made variously from cocoa beans, fruit kernels, coffee beans, nuts and vanilla beans. Best known are Crème de Cacao, made by maceration or percolation of the Venezuelan cocoa beans, and marketed as a colourless or brown liqueur; Tia Maria, flavoured with Blue Mountain coffee extracts in Jamaican cane spirit; Kahlua, a Mexican coffee liqueur, very popular in the USA; Crème de Vanille, from vanilla beans; and Crème de Noisettes, made from hazelnuts.

Advocaat, a thick custard-like liqueur, made from yolk of egg and grape brandy, is anomalous among liqueurs and cannot be classified with any other. Its strength of 30° proof is the lowest among liqueurs, and for this reason it once had its own Customs category. The Dutch advocaats are the best known.

Classification of French liqueurs

The French are meticulous in the classification of their wines, and the principle has been extended to include their liqueurs.

A simple liqueur is a sweetened spirit which must contain 20 kg of sugar per 100 litres of liqueur. The *demi-fines* must have a standard strength of 40° proof, with 20 to 25 kg of sugar per 100 litres of liqueur. *Fines* and *surfines* must have standard strengths of 49° and 52° proof respectively, the former with 40 to 45 kg and the latter 45 to 50 kg sugar per 100 litres.

'Double liqueurs', though theoretically containing 100% increase in flavouring agents, more usually contain only a 50% increase. This is because certain oils, if present in greater proportions, tend to cloud the liqueurs when water is added.

Other definitions applying to liqueurs are *triple-sec*, a misleading term applied loosely to curaçaos which have been doubly rectified; *ratafias*, originally liqueurs drunk at the ratification of treaties or agreements, but latterly meaning liqueurs based on wine spirits; *eis-liköre*, for German liqueurs intended for drinking 'on the rocks'; and *kristal-liköre* and *millefiori*, for German and Italian liqueurs containing sugar crystals.

Liqueurs play their part in the kitchen, but because of their natural sweetness, are used mainly for embellishing sweet courses. The more famous recipes include Triple Sec for crêpes suzettes, Grand Marnier for soufflés, Maraschino for compôte des fruits, and Crème de Noisettes for hazelnut meringues. Liqueurs do however, find their way into fish dishes and entrées. Homard Flambé, cooked with Trappistine and flamed and basted with a mixture of Trappistine and brandy, is a delectable dish. Poulet Vallée d'Auge – a chicken prepared for four and blazed with Calvados (strictly a fruit brandy), is superb. And kebabs, brushed with a mixture of oil and Pernod before cooking, and basted with the resultant marinade, give an excellent variation to the usual flavours.

To do justice to the story of liqueurs in a single chapter is impossible, for the romance behind a hundred of the world's most famous liqueurs would fill a hundred books. It is enough to say that the liqueur's *raison d'être* lies in its digestive qualities, and there can be no more elegant coda to a good dinner.

Beers and brewing

Whatever the Romans came to England for, it was not the beer. They were apparently somewhat surprised to find the natives drinking a fermented liquor made from barley and wheat, and that the practice was by then long established. Barley was cropped by the Britons some 3000 years earlier; their grains had come from Egypt, whence the Britons had also learned the art of brewing.

The Romans did not appear to have cared for the raw drink of the Britons, and certainly ignored it in their chronicles. Ale, mead from honey, and cider from apples were all established as beverages, though ale may only have been available in the southern half of England, where climate and soil were more suitable for growing barley. As with wine, it was the church which established the brewery in the layout of the monasteries, and slowly, as ecclesiastical and moot law was written, ales came to take their position in the developing civilization.

By the end of the seventh century there were three different ales: clear ale, mild ale, and Welsh ale, the latter being a form of *bragawd* in which honey, cinnamon and cloves were among the ingredients. Whether these beverages were available at the earliest inns set up for travellers is not known, but ale-houses and taverns certainly came into the picture during the eighth and ninth centuries, and were sited not only in the cities but also along the old Roman roads. Most were no more than very primitive huts beside the house of the brewer. In the tenth century, King Edgar's Archbishop, Dunstan, decreed that these ale-houses be limited to one per village, thereby giving status to those surviving. It was Dunstan who in 959 decreed 'There shall be one system of measurement, and one standard of weights such as is in use in London and Winchester.' Whether the law was fully effective is doubtful, for it was revised in Magna Carta, but it dates the probable beginnings of capacity measurement.

By the eleventh century the Britons had settled down to an administrative system of law and order. The country was sub-divided and ruled by King, church and squire, who together were to fashion the English way of life. And much of that has evolved round the most famous English drink of all – beer. At the end of the twelfth century, under King Henry II, ale was taxed for the first time, and at about the same time, the Common Council of the Corporation of London decreed at Guildhall that ale-houses in the City be licensed and be built of stone, against the risk of fire.

Now, 2000 million pints of beer are consumed throughout the world every week. After the United States and Germany, Britain is the third largest consumer and accounts for some 10% of the lot, equivalent to three and a half pints a week *per capita* – man, woman and child. The importance of the industry and of the product must therefore not be underrated. The proprietor-ship of the independent brewers throughout the country has steadily fallen into the hands of national combines during the twentieth century; in the ten years to 1973 the number of independents fell from just under two hundred to about eighty. All the other independents – and at the beginning of the twentieth century there were 6,000 of them – are now in the hands of some half-dozen national groups. This evolution has naturally revolu-tionized production methods and equipment, for beer is now mass-produced and marketed in cans as well as bottles and kegs. But the fundamental process of producing beers remains the same.

Beers, by definition, are fermented drinks deriving their alcoholic content from the conversion of malt sugars into alcohol by brewer's yeast. Basically beers are made from barley, yeast, hops and water. Sugar and cereals may be added, and in recent years it has been possible to adjust the very important mineral content of the water, which originally determined the siting of breweries, as for example in Burton-on-Trent and Dublin.

Beers are produced in three main categories. The first is Ales, which may be Pale, Dark or Strong; the second, Stouts, which may be Sweet or Bitter; and the third is Lagers. The barman may be forgiven his confusion when asked merely for 'a beer', as so often happens. All of these beers share the same early treatment in their manufacture, and their alcoholic content is very much the same, except for those specifically described as strong. Draught bitter, light ale, stout and lager all average $3 \cdot 5\%$ to 4% of alcohol by volume, although in different brands they may vary below or above these figures. Pale ales however can have as much as $6 \cdot 5\%$ alcohol, strong lager 8% and strong ale as much as 10%.

The manufacture of beer

The manufacture of beer starts with the malting of barley, and although the process has been mechanized in the giant plants of today, it is best understood by following the original art of the maltster, which is still practised by some small independent producers. Barley is the best cereal for the purpose for several reasons. The foremost reason is that barley produces malt of the best flavour. Secondly, barley husks form a filter bed during the mashing stage of the malting process, and neither wheat nor maize have this husk. Wheat is also unfavourable as an alternative because the wheat germ breaks easily and will tend to form moulds in the mash. Whatever other cereals are used, barley is supreme.

The malting process requires considerable skill. It is carried out in 'maltings', special premises attached to breweries or situated in barley-growing areas. The maltster soaks the barley in water for about sixty hours, following which the barley is spread on the floor of the maltings to germinate. This part of the process is called 'flooring', and what is actually happening during germination is the conversion of the insoluble starch in the barley into soluble sugar. The temperature must be controlled very care-fully during the ten days of flooring and the maltster will rake the barley continuously for this purpose. At the end of this period, the germination will have converted most of the starch into sugar, and should be stopped from going further. The green malt is 'screened' to clean off the culm (small roots that have grown during the flooring) and is then loaded into a kiln to stop the germination and cure the malt. In this drying process the characteristic half-nutty, half-biscuit aroma of the malt develops. According to the type of beer to be made, the malt is kilned to a greater or lesser degree, producing malts of different colours and flavours. The main types, in increasing intensity of colour, are white, crystal, amber and chocolate malt. The last gives colour to stouts.

This in its simplest terms is the process of malting. Brewers rate the quality of malt so produced above that of the malt extracts which save the brewer the time, space and labour involved in the malting process.

The malt is next crushed by mills which have been minutely adjusted, so that the barley grains are crushed without being ground down to flour; at this stage the malt assumes the name 'grist' and goes on a conveyor belt to the grist case to await mashing.

The grist is now mashed with hot liquor in a mash tun. The liquor is water of correct mineral balance. In the mash tun the diastase in the malt converts the starch remaining in the grist to sugar, together with that of unmalted cereals such as flaked maize. At the same time the sugar dissolves in the hot liquor. After a period of one and a half to two hours, the sugar liquid, known as 'wort' (pronounced 'wert') is drained off through slotted plates at the bottom of the mash tun. These slotted plates retain the solid remains of the grist, which still contain some sugar; this sugar is recovered by 'sparging' – spraying the grains with hotter liquor. This further wort is drawn off to join the first, and the spent 'brewer's grains' are sold as cattle food. The wort passes

Fig. 35

The Brewing Process

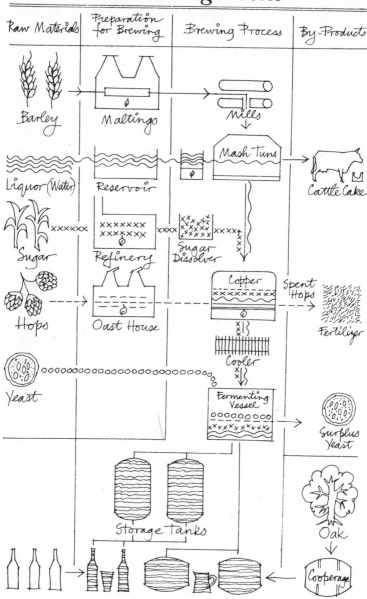

Raw Materials	Preparation for Brewing	Brewing Process	By-Products
Barley	Maltings	Mills	
Liquor (Water)	Reservoir	Mash Tuns	Cattle Cake
Sugar	Refinery	Sugar Dissolver	
Hops	Oast House	Copper	Spent Hops / Fertiliser
Yeast		Cooler / Fermenting Vessel	Surplus Yeast
		Storage Tanks	Oak / Cooperage

on to the copper, which is a circular vessel of copper or stainless steel, where hops and any sugar that may be required are added. Hops are added to give flavour to the beer, and the tannin in them helps to preserve it. They contain no sugar and are nothing to do with the production of alcohol.

The hop is one of a family of perennial plants belonging to the genus *humulus*, which also includes the nettle. The part of the hop used in brewing is the core, which fruits from the female flower and which is two to four inches long with overlapping scales, pale green in colour. The hop fields, called hop gardens in south-east England and hop yards in the west Midlands, need careful husbanding from early spring until late August, when picking begins. As soon as the hops are picked they must be carefully dried with hot air. This takes place in 'oasthouses', and many original ones may still be seen lending charm to the English countryside. The tapering roof of the traditional oasthouse was capped by a pivoting wooden cowl which was designed to stop the back-draught in windy weather. The hops are spread on the porous oasthouse floors, through which hot air rises; after twelve hours they are dry and are then packed in 'pockets', long sacks in which they will be delivered to the brewer. The selection of the right variety of hop is important to the brewer. It will affect the aroma, flavour and resin content of the beer. There are a number of English hops, the more important being the Fuggle and Golding varieties. The bitterness of the hop comes from the resin and aromatic oils of the lupulin – the golden dust found at the base of the hop flower petals.

The hops then, are introduced to the brewing process in the copper. The wort has been run from the mash tun through a tank called the 'underback' or 'wort safe', and on to the copper. The wort and hops are boiled for about two hours; firstly to extract the resin and oils from the hops, and secondly to sterilize the wort. The enzyme diastase, no longer required, is destroyed. Thirdly, the specific gravity of the wort is controlled by the boiling time, during which water will evaporate. Also, during this process unwanted impurities are precipitated or evaporated. In the giant breweries there are coppers with capacities up to 250 barrels, heated by steam coil.

The wort is run off from the copper into a 'hop back'. Here the spent hops and impurities sink to the bottom. When the hop back is drained, these residual materials are retained on a false bottom, and are used as fertilizers. The wort next passes to the 'cooler' which, as a heat-exchanger, also preheats the liquor for the next charge of the mash tun. In the cooler, the wort is brought down to a temperature of about 16°C (61°F) in preparation for the essential yeast activity in the next stage. As the wort goes into the fermentation vessel, the Government becomes interested in excise duty, and each charge must have its volume and specific gravity, 'the Original Gravity', recorded in the Excise Charge Book.

Fermentation in brewing has precisely the same object as in wine and spirit manufacture: to convert sugars into alcohol and carbon dioxide. Brewer's yeast, used for the fermentation, is a cultivated version of *saccharomyces cerevisiae*. It is mixed and added soon after the wort starts running into the fermenting vessels. As fermentation progresses the gravity reduces, and the temperature rises. Cooling coils are fitted in the fermenting vessels to keep the ferment at the correct temperature. This may be done equally effectively by running cold water over the external walls of the vessel, which also makes cleaning easier. Fermentation of beers and stouts takes three to four days, during which gravities and temperature are constantly measured by the brewer. During the process of producing these non-lager beers, a frothy head starts to form inside the fermenting vessel. This is composed of flocculating yeast cells. The head undergoes visual changes which enable the brewer to check the progress of fermentation. When the yeast head is fully formed it is skimmed off and pressed to produce a valuable by-product. The yeast has been multiplying during fermentation, and the quantity of yeast removed in this way will amount to up to five times the quantity put in. The pick of the yeast crops are carefully set aside in cold storage, ready to ferment subsequent brews. This yeast used for production of ales and stouts is known as 'top yeast', because it rises to the top of the fermenting vessel.

In lager production a different yeast, *saccharomyces carlsberg-ensis*, is used. This is known as 'bottom yeast', because it sinks to the bottom of the fermenting vessel rather than rising to the top. Fermentation of lager takes place at a much lower temperature, therefore taking much longer: after primary fermentation, the beer is run into lagering vessels at a temperature between 2°C and 3°C (36°F and 37°F) or even lower. Lagers remain in tank for conditioning and 'chill-proofing' for two to six months, and according to marketing policy, may be carbonated. They are best served chilled, too.

Ales and stouts coming from the fermenting vessel are allowed to settle for a day or two in racking tanks before filling into casks or cellar tanks. Draught beer is perishable, but bottled, canned and container beers are stabilized. Cellar treatments of beer include 'fining' 'priming', 'conditioning' and 'dry hopping'. The clarifying process of fining is done by the addition of isin-glass fining solution. Priming is the addition of sugar solution to sweeten the finished beer, and conditioning is carbonation to increase liveliness. Dry hopping is the addition of a small quantity of choice hops to the cask of finished beer in order to increase the delicate hop flavour and aroma of the beer.

The modern process of brewing follows all the development stages of the original malting, mashing, sparging, boiling with hops and fermenting with yeast. Equipment has been introduced to check and control the physical conditions throughout the process, and also to make the process a continuous one, with raw materials being fed in at appropriate stages, and beer flowing continuously from the fermentation vessels into racking tanks.

Beers for sale in bulk are put up in hygienic containers known always as casks. Today the traditional oak casks have virtually disappeared and stainless steel and aluminium casks have taken their place. They are of varying sizes, their capacities ranging from the 'butt' of 108 gallons (490 litres) down to the 'firkin' of 9 gallons (40 litres) and the 'pin' of $4\frac{1}{2}$ gallons (20 litres). Draught beers reach the public house and other points of sale by tanker or cask. Latterly, sufficient supplies of keg beers, which are chilled and filtered to keep stable, are kept at depots close to the point of sale.

Bottled beers may be matured before or after bottling. A bottle of beer contains about double its own volume of carbon dioxide gas in solution; its fresh, sparkling appearance and its traditional head in the glass are all due to this gas. Maturation is a continuous process and thus there is a right time to drink beer after bottling.

Bottling plants are highly geared to deal with millions of bottles daily, and yet reject any that are imperfect or unclean. So-called 'bottled' beers are distributed in returnable bottles, non-returnable bottles or cans. These vary in size from the 'nip' of almost 7 fluid ounces (20 centilitres) to the seven pint or gallon cans for parties. The service given by the brewer to the public is both compact and complete.

Anatomy of the trade

To the consumer, this is perhaps the most important chapter of all in the story of the preparation of wines, spirits, liqueurs and beers. For it tells of the massive investment, the implicit crafts and skills, the infinite care and patience, and the deep sense of responsibility of the world industries involved in the process of bringing these products to the market-place. Together they represent the guarantees of quality and description of the contents of the bottle offered for sale.

Marketing

The marketing operation is an international one, and involves not only the producers but many allied industries, such as bottle and cork manufacturers, coopers, rail, road and sea transport operators, insurance brokers and operators of warehouse services, lawyers and accountants. There are also those who act as wholesalers, and retailers selling direct to the consumer. The trade is international, and the journey from producer to consumer may be long or short.

The short journey is made where a large wine merchant owns vineyards, bottles in his own cellars and sells the wine through his own retail outlets: in much the same way, large brewing groups sell their own beer in their tied public houses. The long journey is made where a small proprietor sells his wine through a broker, either in bottle or in cask, to a *négoçiant*, from whom a shipper in England buys the wine and imports it, selling it to his customers. These may be the wine divisions of large brewing groups, small off-licence traders, hotels and restaurants or favoured individuals. There can be a short journey from the small proprietor too, for many a Frenchman buys a cask of wine from a little vineyard that he knows, and bottles it himself at home. Of course, it may not be so well bottled, but it will have cost him less.

Within the trade, the existence of organizations created by those sharing mutual interests goes back and is lost in time. In England, four of the ancient Livery Companies of the City of London received their charters from the Crown for watching over different aspects of the industry – the Vintners, Distillers, Brewers and Innholders: in France, the 'Courtiers Picquet en Vin', the ancient and honourable body of wine-brokers, received their charter from Philippe le Bon in the fourteenth century. These traditional organizations still have a role to play in the modern operation.

A measure often used in the sale of wine from the larger vineyards, in Bordeaux particularly, is the *tonneau*. This is a measure amounting to four *barriques* or hogsheads each of 50 gallons (225 litres). The wine sold in this fashion is not necessarily sold in bulk, but frequently in bottle, the *tonneau* being 96 dozen bottles. Some of the most famous owners of the Médoc test the market by offering a portion of their production (a *tranche*) at a fixed price per *tonneau* – which will be a high one. Depending on the response to his offer, the great owner will offer further *tranches* at a higher or lower price. Meanwhile, of course, all the other growers who employ this method will have had to guess the success of his offer, and offer their own wines at appropriate prices, bearing in mind their status in relation to the first. Rather like horse-racing, and doubtless just as exciting.

But there are many owners who bottle at domaine or château and sell to *négociants*, who appear at different levels in the marketing strata, and indeed many vineyards are owned by *négociants* who may bottle at château or in their cellars in the towns. Other vineyards may be owned by hotels or trading groups; for instance Château Loudenne in the Médoc, which has been in the hands of Gilbey SA longer than any other property in Bordeaux has been under one owner. In much the same way, the production and sale of spirits varies from the giant international distilling groups to the small grower in Cognac, who keeps a few casks of his own distillation at home until funds are needed for a family wedding or funeral (and such casks are highly valued by the great Cognac houses).

Few of the basic producers of wine and spirits dispose of their merchandise without the services of a broker, whose job it is to assess the produce where it is made, and to introduce it to the *négoçiant*. In France, this is still the role of the *courtier*. The broker takes his commission on the actual sale of the wine or spirit, and may not deal on his own behalf. Usually it is the *négoçiant* who buys: his full title is *négoçiant-éleveur*, for he is responsible not only for buying wines and spirits, but also for shipping or marketing them. Wines may come to his cellars in bulk containers, road and rail tankers and a variety of other containers. His main task is looking after young wines until they are ready to be bottled – raising them like children – and this is just what *éleveur* means: teacher.

Some of the wines bought by the *négoçiant* will be unable to stand in the market on their own, and will need to be blended. Blending is a great art, demanding a critical and well-trained palate. The aim of the blender is to make two or more insufficient wines balance their faults and virtues to produce a better wine, meaning one that sells. The *négoçiant* will finally sell his wines at home, or export them in bulk, or both.

The representatives of the shippers from the importing countries will pay frequent visits to the *négoçiants*, whose agents they are, to taste the wines, discuss prices, and arrange details of shipment. Or, if their agency agreements allow, they may look around to find wines which will be good value for their customers. Such men need to have a good knowledge of markets, costing practice, and shipping and customs procedures, as well as a discerning and objective palate.

The importer will use the services of UK shipping and forwarding agents, whose particular expertise in shipping, documentation, and the entry, clearance, and insurance of such parcels, represents a considerable saving of manpower in the modern economy. Having received the wine into his bonded warehouse, and after satisfying himself that the wine is acceptable, the shipper will have to decide if it needs any treatment. Wine does not like being jerked about in travel or subjected to sudden changes in temperature, and will require time to rest after its journey. Moreover, it may have contracted some sickness on its travels: a cask may have had a faulty stave, which would give the wine a 'woody' taste: or the lining of a Safrap container may have been damaged, allowing the wine to come in contact with iron, resulting in a greyish haze and possibly a smell of bad eggs. These faults can be cured, but their cure requires a diagnosis and treatment just as skilled as the doctor's in treating his human patients.

Once the wine is rested and cured of any sickness, it is ready for the next stage. If it arrived in bottle it can be sent out to the wholesaler or retailer, after checking samples for quality; if samples of a wine bottled at source, abroad, show signs of secondary fermentation in bottle, the whole consignment will have to be disgorged, filtered, and rebottled in sterile bottles. The British trade has always been renowned for its skill in bottling, and attempts of foreign agencies to enforce bottling at source have always been resisted. If the wine is ordinary wine in bulk, it may require blending. Just as people in unison can produce something greater than any one of them on his own, so can individual, perhaps even nondescript, wines be blended into something better: the shipper's skill lies here, in his vision of the final product when purchasing its components. Having decided on his blend, the shipper makes it.

The next link in the chain is the wholesaler, who may in fact be the shipper himself. Now, having the United Kingdom particularly in mind, licences should be mentioned. The wholesaler must possess a dealer's excise licence for selling quantities over two gallons (nine litres) or one dozen bottles of wine (for beer and cider the equivalents are four and a half

Opposite: Exterior, Oasthouses

gallons (twenty litres) and two dozen bottles). In the UK, retailers selling for consumption off the premises require a Justices' licence. Establishments which sell wines, spirits and beers direct to the public on the premises also require a Justices' licence; but they are subject, in the UK, to special controls imposed for social reasons. The hours when alcohol may be consumed are laid down, and so are the persons to whom it may be sold: no person under 18 may buy or consume alcohol in a bar, nor may he serve in one. The licensee must be of good character, and must not allow his premises to be used as a resort of criminals or prostitutes. Drunkenness observed on the premises can cost him his licence. He may obtain an extension of hours to his licence on special occasions: he may obtain an occasional licence to cover a dance, or 'wine and cheese party' in another location where wine is to be sold. But every occasion when alcoholic beverages are sold for consumption requires a licence. There are variants of the full on-licence, such as the club licence, the restaurant licence, and the residential licence for guests at hotels and boarding houses, each restricting service to a particular class of customer. On-licences also specify the exact premises, down to the room in a house, where alcohol may be consumed. And even this does not end the list of licences required for different purposes. In the UK, distillers must have an excise licence (for no matter what quantity or distillate), and brewers require a brewers' licence.

As soon as the sugary wort or must starts to ferment and becomes alcoholic, further processing must, by law, be continued under Crown lock – on warehouse, washback, still or spirit safe. The home brewer or wine-maker in the UK is exempt from licence, provided he produces only for the use of his own household.

We have seen that there can be a long chain between the producer and the customer. Some large groups of companies have been formed in the trade to encompass this vertically: they are, at the same time, vineyard owners, *négociants-éleveurs*,

Opposite: Interior of a typical Off-Licence

shippers, wholesalers and retailers. On a smaller scale, the shipper can be found who runs a chain of off-licences and also restaurants. Firms also integrate horizontally, in handling wines of several *négoçiants* and countries, together with spirits and liqueurs of various sorts.

Trade associations

A number of international and regional associations exist to protect the trade, and the good name of their products. In some cases they also promote sales. INAO, for example, sponsored by the French Government, protects the reputation of French wines; Consorzi, Juntas and Consejos do the same for other countries and individual regions. The receiving countries also find the need to form associations of particular interests. In the UK, there are associations of Champagne shippers, of brandy shippers, of sherry shippers, of Cyprus wine shippers, of gin distillers and rectifiers and of rum importers, to name but a few. Their members come together for mutual assistance and protection. Similarly, there are regional associations of wine-merchants, who resolve local matters between themselves, besides presenting the views of local trade and consumer interests to the national association. This national association – the Wine and Spirit Association of Great Britain – represents the views of the British trade at large to the Government, especially in the fields of taxation and customs procedure, and has daily contact with Government departments and with Parliament on these and any other matters affecting the trade: it passes on the results of its investigations and representations to its subscribing members. Subscriptions are required because this work costs money, and the individual firms who benefit must pay for the service. The service is so valuable that no firm of any worth would consider not belonging. It is not the only national association: there are the Scotch Whisky Association, the Brewers' Society, the National Federation of Off-Licencees, and others which reflect particular national interests. All of these keep in close contact with one another and coordinate their efforts as far as possible, so that uniform opinion may be presented to the Government.

Three more service organizations in Britain should be mentioned here: the Wine Development Board, which promotes public interest in wines and spirits and educates the consumer; the Wine and Spirit Education Trust, set up by the Vintners' Company and the Wine and Spirit Association of Great Britain to improve the knowledge of people engaged in the wine and spirit and associated trades; and the Wine Standards Board, set up by the Vintners' Company with Government approval, to control the proper documentation of imported wine.

On the international scale, there are more associations. Since Britain's entry into the European Economic Community, there are now more wine-importing than wine-producing countries in the Community, so an EEC wine-importing countries group has been formed. There is also an EFTA wine-merchants group. On the global scale, there is an International Federation of Wine and Spirit Merchants, who hold an annual Congress in various parts of the world to discuss such matters as international labelling regulations, the substances which should be permitted to be added to wines and spirits, and professional education of the merchant.

Governmental control

Perhaps it is through the eyes of the Government inspector that a review of some wine and spirits standards and constraints can best be observed. Firstly, he will know the Government departments who share the responsibility of administering the law. The most important ministry today is the Ministry of Agriculture, Fisheries and Food, but other ministries such as the Department of Health and the Home Office will be concerned in the administration of certain Acts.

The labelling requirements are affected by the Customs and Excise Act, the Food and Drugs Act and the Labelling of Food Orders made under it, the Weights and Measures Act, the Trade

Descriptions Act, the Anglo-Portuguese Trade Treaties Acts
and a wealth of case law. Labels now constantly need to conform
with new international agreements, binding EEC, EFTA and
other grouped countries. The Customs officer will need to know
and to be able to recognize on sight the different containers for
wines and spirits, and know their capacities. Particular attention
will be given by him and the Weights and Measures inspector
to the alcoholic strengths in relation to taxation and to the
claims made on the label.

Reference has been made to the activities of wine-makers,
brokers, *négoçiants*, shippers, importers, wholesalers and retailers,
and in the context of these references, two things have not been
mentioned. Both are very important. Firstly, the wine which is
the subject of a series of deals along the line is rarely, if ever,
bought, sold and passed on immediately. Sometimes years elapse
before a consignment of wine passes from one stage to the next.
There are wines which have been lying in bond in the London
docks for over 50 years. Secondly, before any deal is made, the
wine is tasted. The method of tasting will bear careful examination and is most interesting. A large volume of wine changes
hands at wine sales, where professional tasting is the key to the
bidding. While there is room for the talented amateur on such
occasions, the uninitiated buyer who does not know how to taste
objectively and value a wine, can get his fingers burnt.

Everyone should know how to taste, in order to gain the
maximum benefit from each mouthful. Wines and spirits are
expensive, and it is a pity to pour them down the throat without
fully appreciating them, and the work of all those who have
brought them from vineyard or distillery. The grower tastes, as
he makes his wine, to see that it is progressing favourably and is
not getting sick. The broker, *négoçiant* and importer will all
taste the wine to see that it will suit their purposes. The shipper
will also taste as he blends wines together, to see that they suit his
market. The importer will taste a sample from each cask on
arrival, to see that the quality is up to the sample that he tasted in

the vineyard region. The wholesale or retail buyer tastes to select suitable wines for his customers.

Tasting, to the layman, might infer drinking, but this is not so. 'Testing' could be a better term. Tasting is used as a judgement of quality and soundness, but it does not only involve the sense of taste – wine also has to be seen, smelt and felt.

First then, sight. If a wine does not look bright – if it is hazy or has an unnatural colour – it is unlikely to taste good and the taster is unlikely to let it into his mouth. If that test is not passed, the taster would proceed with the utmost caution. Clarity tells that the wine is wholesome and colour can help to tell its age. Wine that is young looks fresh in colour, and white wines may turn gold from pale yellow, or possibly from almost white. Red wines start off their life looking a light or a dark purple, depending on where and how they were made. With age, these colours dull gradually, so that a very old red wine may look the colour of a fine old mahogany table, and an old white wine may look a deep golden colour. If a red wine looks a dirty shade of brown this will indicate that all is not well.

Next, smell the wine. If the wine fails to look bright it is unlikely to smell good, and if it does not smell clean then, once again, the taster is unlikely to let it into his mouth. Sound wines must look sound and smell sound. They should *not* smell of rotten eggs, cabbage, old socks or dirty drying-up cloths. A sick wine can smell of any of these, although the last smell may be just that – from a dirty glass. So the wine-taster will always be careful to see that his glass is well-washed and polished and free of taint.

Fine wines smell strongly. They will have a good bouquet of fruit or spices, and will shout their quality from the roof tops: they smell beautiful. The lesser wines are very good to drink, but do not smell of very much, which is possibly one reason why their price is more reasonable. If wine has a chemical smell which catches the back of the nose, this may be cured by exposure to the air.

After sight and smell have contributed to the diagnosis, the next step is to taste. The palate will normally confirm what the eyes and nose have already discovered. The taster will take a generous mouthful of wine and hold it in his mouth. He will *chew* it, wash his tongue in it, and swirl it round the mouth. He may also draw air through the wine in his mouth to bring out the aroma of the wine. The sense organs of his mouth are distributed between the tongue, the gums and the palate, and they may occur in different places for different people. A wine with a high degree of sweetness, but having a balancing acidity, might well taste too sharp on the tip of the tongue, yet too sweet if poured down the back of the throat. The sides of the tongue and the sides of the mouth detect the bitterness of tannin, particularly in red wines. The gums are quick to detect alcohol, as a prickly sensation. Alcohol, like tannin, is a preservative, and the presence of these indicates that a wine is likely to last well. The 'feel' of the wine in the mouth is also experienced at this time.

While the taster has the wine in his mouth, he should be reaching a conclusion as to whether the wine is balanced, for this is what he is looking for. The wine should be neither too sweet nor too acid, neither too heavy in alcohol nor too light. It should not be flat, and its sweetness and alcohol should be balanced by acid. When his judgement is made, the professional wine-taster will spit out the wine. This he does primarily to remove the memory of the wine in readiness for the next, and a dry biscuit will help him to do this. Young tannic wines, were they swallowed during a tasting, could easily upset the stomach; also the cold sober judgement of the taster could be affected as the day wore on, if wines were swallowed rather than ejected from the mouth.

But there is one quality of a wine which may not be immediately apparent – the quality known as 'finish'. This is the very *character* of the wine, and it is difficult to put into words. If, however, the taster asks himself 'How long can I remember the wine?' he is talking about finish. The memory of a great wine will stay vividly on the palate, possibly for a period of twenty-four hours or more, and will do so in spite of other wines and foods consumed during this time.

These tests come to the merchant's aid when a shipment of wine, or even a single bottle, is unlabelled. The labels may have been washed off, or they may never have existed and the invoice may have been mislaid. Then the taster must ascribe an origin and value to the wine, in order to sell it. In the trade, very few people have to do this, and very few people can. It is an art based on long experience and a phenomenal memory. The reader may be fortunate enough to be invited to one of the tastings held by firms in the trade. Smoking is not permitted: this is not to say that smoking destroys the palate – about half the Masters of Wine are smokers – but non-smokers could not detect anything in a wine if someone were smoking in their presence. For the same reason, ladies invited to trade tastings will attend un-perfumed.

One problem confronting the taster is how to record his sensations: memory is a fickle thing, and the senses of smell and taste, though very evocative, are recessive. It is wise, then, to take notes, at the time if possible, but if not as soon as possible afterwards. In the notes should be recorded the name of the wine, its vintage, the name of the shipper, and the price. Then, impressions of the appearance of the wine, to the eye, to the nose, and to the palate should be noted, ending with a general assessment. The language in which all these things are recorded should be restrained: 'A well-travelled little wine appearing rather above its station' does nothing to describe the wine, but much to describe the author of the remark.

The eye will record clarity, haziness and deposit; it will note the colour of white wines, ranging from white through straw or green, to deep or old gold; and will record the colours of red wines from purple through garnet, to mahogany. As at a presentation of wines all should be star-bright, only the rare exception will call for a remark on clarity.

The nose will record bouquet – of fruit or flower, of spices, of fragrance, and the peppery or baked smell of wines made in hot countries. But the nose must be alert for the sickly sweetness of a wine turning to vinegar, or the acetic smell of one that already has: and for the musty smell of a cask with a faulty stave.

The palate will record alcoholic strength from the pricking on the gums, acid from the tongue, sweetness and tannin from the same organ. These sensations may be described as body, acidity, sweetness, lusciousness or heaviness (of alcohol); and, at this stage, the taster will make up his mind if the wine is balanced, or too acidic or too flat; if the sweetness is counterbalanced by acidity and fruitiness, or the general impression is cloying or nondescript. The tannin content of red wines comes into the computation also: red wines may be hard, with much tannin, or soft, with little.

The finish, which is perhaps determined shortly after tasting, sets the seal on the whole operation: fine wines not only shout their qualities aloud but also stay long in the memory, which is one reason why they are so expensive. And from all this information, the taster must try to price the wine; if at an auction, he must know whether to bid, and to what level; if at an off-licence he must consult his memory and decide whether to buy at the price offered; or if at a restaurant, he must again consult his memory and decide which wine gives the best value for his money.

World output

Every year the world output of wine alone, amounts to the equivalent of some 40,000 million bottles; with the addition of spirits and beers, it can be seen that the alcoholic drinks industry has a turnover well in excess of £1000,000,000 per week. The weight of money and labour involved in the mammoth task of the manufacture and distribution of this great volume of consumable merchandise is enormous, and this short chapter provides a brief sketch of the structure of the trade which manages it.

Wines, spirits and the consumer

The reader will by now have learned much of the variety of wines and spirits, and have been tantalized by the immense range available. He may, by this time, be thirsty, and eager to test his newly-gained knowledge in practice. In this story of the origin and manufacture of wines and spirits, drinking habits have been shown to change with fashion and necessity. But overlying the preferences and constraints of each succeeding generation, there are unchanging reasons for drinking at all. Certainly everyone needs a regular liquid intake merely to live, and for that, pure water will do nicely. However, it is the stimulus of alcohol that appeals to the human being. In tiredness he is revived; in trouble, consoled; in despair, encouraged; in perplexity, inspired; in solitude, befriended; in happiness, uplifted; and in company, he is at home.

There will always be a sound reason for enjoying a drink. Dean Aldrich of Christ Church, Oxford, some two hundred and fifty years ago, had it thus:

> 'If all be true that I do think
> There are five reasons we should drink:
> Good wine – a friend – or being dry,
> Or lest we should be by and by,
> Or any other reason why.'

The Dean may have had his tongue in his cheek, but the gentle scholar nevertheless had the right idea. Wines and spirits are always enjoyable in company, and need no justification. Such drinking translates an occurrence into an occasion, and the intangible power of alcohol which helps people rise to this occasion is perhaps the most telling of its qualities.

Thanks to a helpful, efficient and informed off-licence trade, wines and spirits can be enjoyed in the home as well as in the restaurant, hotel, club or pub. This has become particularly true in recent years, when there are so many chain stores and supermarkets selling wines and spirits; wines can be, and are, picked up with the groceries, and there is no longer any prejudice about the housewife buying them. They are now, in Britain, commonplace items of everyday life – which is not to say that they should be mishandled, misused or unappreciated.

To enjoy wines and spirits to the full, it is necessary to choose the most suitable drink, not only for the occasion, but also for the company.

Selection of drinks

Before meals, for 'a drink before lunch' (meaning that the guest is *not* expected to stay for lunch), or for cocktails, either sherry or mixed drinks are usual. The host can serve gin and tonic, if possible with ice and a slice of lemon, or whisky, remembering to ask if the guest likes soda, water, or ice, and refusing to be shocked if he likes cola with it. It is also well to know the names of some of the more fashionable cocktails, and what goes in them (a short list is given in Appendix 4); the impression that a Martini consisted of equal quantities of gin and brandy has proved to be not only expensive but socially disastrous.

Often, it is better to serve wine, particularly if there are large numbers. Sherry has been mentioned, but this can cloy the palate if more than a couple of glasses are taken. Dry white port, with its fruity flavour, can make a lovely *apéritif* served well chilled. But beverage wines can also suit this sort of occasion perfectly, and there are many to choose from: the white wines of Germany, Austria, Yugoslavia, Hungary, and South Africa are all good. France also produces wines light enough for such parties, and the best one is Champagne, the wine of kings, and the king of wines. But not all our readers are kings, nor as rich as sultans, and Champagne is deservedly expensive, as has been mentioned in an earlier chapter. There are other sparkling wines

which may take its place, to please without undue expense –
Vouvray or Saumur from the Loire, Bourgogne Mousseux, Asti
Spumante from Italy and branded wines from France and Spain –
speaking for the western hemisphere. Here is a recipe, from
Germany originally, for a summer drink.

The night before a lunchtime party, take 1 lb ($\frac{1}{2}$ kg) of strawberries, fresh cherries, or sliced peaches and lay them in a bowl.
Cover them with caster sugar. In the morning, add one bottle
of dry white wine and $\frac{1}{3}$ bottle of brandy. When the guests
arrive, add two more bottles of dry white wine, a bottle of
sparkling wine, and a large bottle of soda-water. Stir and serve.
This will give about thirty glasses.

With meals, there is a whole panorama of wines to choose from,
which may be indeed embarrassingly large for the uninitiated.
Generally speaking, the rule is to drink what one likes, or what
one knows one's guests like, which may not be the same thing.
But there are a few tips which may be helpful about wines that
do not go well with certain foods. With savoury dishes, sweet
white wines can be very cloying. Fish makes a tannic red wine
taste metallic. Because of the sulphur in eggs, they rarely go well
with red wine. And cream cheeses, such as Camembert or Brie,
can make some white wines, particularly those from the Rhineland, taste very nasty indeed. Apart from these warnings, some
generally-accepted suggestions can be made for matching wines
with food, and these will be useful either when choosing wines
for guests or when recommending wines for customers whose
particular tastes are unknown. The light dry wines suitable as
apéritifs will also complement shellfish and the lighter white
fish; but for heavier or oilier fish, such as salmon, sole or halibut,
a more full-bodied dry white wine will stand up to the food
better. These wines will also complement veal, pork or chicken
dishes. Light dry white wines tend to be paler in colour than the
full-bodied ones, which is a rough guide when buying ordinary
'table wines'. The following are a few selected 'quality wines'
of the EEC which fall into these two categories:

Light Dry White

> FRANCE: Chablis, from Burgundy; Muscadet, Sancerre or Pouilly Blanc Fumé, from the Loire; Brut Champagne.
> GERMANY: Moselles.
> ITALY: Verdicchio, from Marche; Frascati from Lazio.

Full-Bodied White

> FRANCE: Meursault or other Côte de Beaune, from Burgundy; White Graves or Entre-deux-Mers, from Bordeaux; Alsace wines; Condrieu or Hermitage, from the Rhône valley.
> GERMANY: Rheingau, Rheinhessen or Nahe.
> ITALY: Soave, from Veneto; Orvieto Secco, from Umbria.

Also in the full-bodied white category are the wines of Austria, the Rieslings of Lutomer in Yugoslavia and Balaton in Hungary, the white Riojas of Spain and many more, too numerous to detail, from all parts of the world. Australia, South Africa, Argentina, Chile and California all produce fine white wines, both light and full-bodied.

The lighter meats may also be complemented by the lighter red wines. Examples are young Chianti from Italy, young Beaujolais from Southern Burgundy, and the rare red wines of Chinon and Bourgueil in the Loire Valley. And, not far removed from the lighter red wines, are rosé wines, although these vary considerably in sweetness and body. The rosé of Tavel in the Southern Rhône valley and the rosés of Bordeaux and Southern Portugal will be good with white meats. The rosés of Anjou and the semi-sparkling rosés of Northern Portugal are sweeter and for some palates might clash with savoury dishes. Well chilled, however, they are perfect for picnics.

Roast beef and game, and game birds, are full in flavour, and would make the light red wines and all but the biggest and most full-bodied white wines taste insipid. These meats therefore need a heavier red wine, just as red wines, with their extra tannin content, need robust foods to complement them. Although all red wines are normally put up in coloured bottles, to avoid their colour being affected by light, it is usually possible to assess the density of the colour by holding the bottle up against the light. Generally speaking, the denser the colour, the heavier and more tannic the wine will be. These wines can be hard when young; that is to say, some of the tannin gives a harsh texture to the wine in the mouth. This can often be alleviated by exposing the wine to air for a short time, by decanting. As wine ages, the excess tannin is precipitated as a deposit, which lies at the bottom of the bottle.

There are many fine red wines to choose from in Europe. Among the more expensive are the château-bottled clarets of Bordeaux, the fine Burgundies from the Côte d'Or, Châteauneuf-du-Pape from the southern Rhône, the fine red Riojas of Spain and the Barolos and Barbarescos of Italy. In the middle price range are the ordinary Bordeaux, Burgundy, and Rhône wines, and a number of wines with unfamiliar names from the Midi region of France. The labels of some of these wines may bear the letters AC or VDQS as a mark of quality. From Italy, Valpolicella and Bardolino are in the same price range as the older Chianti, which is made to lay down as well as to drink when young. Such Italian wines would be labelled DOC. Red wines are particularly suited to accompany cheeses, especially English cheeses. The French usually take cheese before the sweet course so that they can first enjoy what remains of their robust red wine, which will not taste the same after sweet food.

There is another range of wines to draw from for the sweet course – the sweet white wines, particularly those that have been made from 'noble rot' grapes. For very special occasions there are the expensive Sauternes from Bordeaux, the Beerenausleses and Trockenbeerenausleses from Alsace and Germany, Ausbruch wines from Austria and Tokay from Hungary. For lesser celebrations, the white Italian wines marked *abboccato* from Orvieto, wine from Panadés in Spain (until recently possibly called 'Spanish Sauternes'), or a sweet white Graves from Bordeaux, are all excellent for this purpose; those with sweeter preferences could happily drink any of them throughout a meal.

With nuts, or as in England with the cheese at the end of the meal, the great dessert wines come into their own. Port – truly the Englishman's wine – and Bual and Malmsey Madeiras are wines for drinking great toasts with, and for sipping gently through sometimes interminable speeches. It is customary at this stage to place the decanters on the table, leaving each diner to help himself. Traditionally the decanters are passed to the left, after the host has helped himself; one way only, so that the decanters don't all get stuck at one end, and to the left, because most people are right-handed and the glasses are always placed to the diner's right. Pity the poor left-hander who has to reach across – and pity also the principal guest on the host's right hand: a good host will pour wine for this guest before he passes the decanter.

At Lloyds in London there is a collection of Nelson relics, including a coaster in the shape of a jolly boat given by Nelson to the Master of the 'Victory'. There is a story that when the port in this silver coaster got stuck at one end of the mess table the officers would cry 'Push out the boat' to get it under way again: the origin of a happy expression.

Finally, with the coffee, *digestif* spirits and liqueurs may be offered. If ladies are present, they will probably have withdrawn to another room, where the men will later join them: thus they may enjoy their liqueurs while the men are finishing their port, and be spared the boredom of hearing their husbands' stories mistold yet once more.

Labelling regulations
What should one look for when buying wines? First, a good supplier – one who knows his wines and his customers, and who can therefore make sound suggestions for their enjoyment. If

he is right, they will return to buy again. But if the customer finds himself in a strange town, he is left to his own devices. His choice will be narrowed by knowing what sort of wine he wants, but even then there may be a confusingly large range on offer. That is why wines and spirits are labelled. And, to protect the consumer, they have to be, by law.

First of all, the label must contain an 'appropriate description': 'Whisky', 'Gin', 'Rum', 'Vermouth', and 'Sherry' are all 'appropriate descriptions'. So are the names of wines, and if those names are the names of EEC quality wines, such as Nuits St. Georges, Côtes-du-Rhône, or Bordeaux, they must *be* those wines, and have the letters AC or AOC, meaning Appellation Contrôlée, or VDQS, meaning superior wines from a legally-delimited area, on the label. In Italy, quality wines are labelled DOC or DOCG [*Denominazione d'Origine Controllata (e Garantita)*], while in Germany they would be labelled *Qualitätswein*, or *Qualitätswein mit Prädikat*. Nor can any other wines be labelled similarly, with intent to deceive. 'Spanish Sauternes' is not now a permitted labelling, nor would 'Shablee' be acceptable. The next item that must appear on the label is the name and address of the shipper or bottler, for if there is any fault with the wine or spirit, it must lie at his door and, if it has caused any sickness, he is liable to pay damages. Should anything which should not be there be found in the bottle, on analysis by the Weights and Measures inspectors, the bottler is liable for prosecution on account of the harmful substance. But on the credit side, his is the name to look for, because the name of a reputable shipper is a guarantee that the wine or spirit will be good value for money, particularly when the name of the wine is a brand name unfamiliar to the customer. In the past, any over-production in the quality wine areas could be sold in the UK under the same name as the limited quantity entitled to the name in its country of origin, but without the letters AC. Now that this is no longer legal, the shipper will put it up under a brand name bearing no relation to the quality wine name. The customer who trusts his shipper, and knows his brand names, can get a wonderful bargain.

Another item which must appear on the label is the country or countries of origin of the wine or spirit, for this enables a faulty product to be traced back to its source. So the customer may find that his latest bottle of branded wine bears the words 'Produce of Italy' while the last bottle of the same brand bore the words 'Produce of Austria, Hungary and Yugoslavia'. Does this matter? Not at all, for it means that the shipper who blended the wine has found that he can make his standard blend better, at that time, from the wines of Italy than he could from the wines of the other countries. Having regard to the element of luck in every year, this is not surprising, and the customer should merely be grateful for the skill of the blender.

One important matter to be remembered in connection with blended wines is that the label of a blend of quality wines may not show any classification higher than the common name to which all constituents of the blend would be entitled. Thus, a blend of Gevrey-Chambertin and Chambolle-Musigny could not be entitled to any name higher than Bourgogne Rouge. A blend of Médoc and St. Emilion could only be called Bordeaux, or Bordeaux Supérieur if its alcoholic strength exceeded $11 \cdot 5°$GL.

On ordinary wines, the strength does not have to appear on the label at present, although it may have to in the future; but this information does have to appear on the labels of spirits and liqueurs or of wines for which special tonic or other properties are claimed. This also applies to 'wines' made from fruit other than grapes, or from a mixture of fruits. In the UK, the strength is shown in degrees proof: on the continent it is shown in degrees Gay-Lussac, equivalent to percentages of alcohol by volume.

Choosing from a wine list

The label gives the consumer a great deal of information, but it will not usually tell him what the liquid inside the bottle is going to look or taste like: only experience, or the advice of the seller, can do that. Much has been said about buying wines from the off-licence, store or supermarket: but most customers will gain their experience in a restaurant to begin with. The wine list can be just as confusing as the array of bottles in a store; but the wine waiter, particularly if he wears the badge of the Guild of Sommeliers, can give as good advice as the manager of an off-licence.

What has been said about wines with food may have given some guidance on what part of the wine list to examine. But what should the host do if all his party have ordered different foods – some fish, some steaks, some game? There are several ways of tackling the problem. The normal bottle contains six glasses, and a half-bottle, three: and with a reasonably-sized meal, a half-bottle of beverage wine is not excessive for one person. So, if there are two diners, and one orders sole and the other steak, why not have a half-bottle of red wine and a half-bottle of white? The same solution applies if both have fish followed by meat, but then the sommelier should be told when to serve the wines. Another solution is to choose a wine that can be drunk all through the meal, one which will go with anything. The white wines of Alsace are an excellent example, as they will complement every food, even strong creamy cheeses, and the same applies to the white wines of Germany, Austria, Hungary and Yugoslavia if the stronger cheeses are avoided. Young Beaujolais or Chianti, being very light on the palate, can be all-purpose wines except for shellfish or sweets. And for those who can afford it, Champagne has always been the wine for every occasion and every food. With oysters, with duck, or with Brie, Champagne tastes delicious.

When the wine has been ordered, the sommelier should bring the bottle without opening it, and show the label to the host so that he may confirm that it is the wine selected. Perhaps 'Chianti Classico – DOC' was ordered; but on inspection, the label includes the words 'Chianti – Denominazione d'Origine Controllata', and not the word 'Classico', which denotes an inner district of higher-quality wines, at an appreciably higher price. Having pointed out to the sommelier that this is not the wine ordered, he will immediately change it for the right one: it is an easy mistake to make, as the difference on the label is so small.

Having agreed the bottle, the sommelier will then remove the foil from the top of the neck, draw the cork, and serve a small portion to the host, so that he can tell that it is sound by its appearance and smell. At this stage, and for this purpose, it is seldom necessary actually to taste the wine. It is fortunately very rare to find a bottle in poor condition – 'corky' wine may be discovered only once in a lifetime, and will probably never reach the customer, because the sommelier will already have smelled the cork and withdrawn the bottle without serving it. However, when first opened, a fine old wine may smell a little musty, but this 'bottle stink' caused by its long imprisonment in the bottle, will soon evaporate with exposure to air. If in doubt, the sample of wine may be poured from one glass to another: if the bad smell fades, all will be well.

Storing wine in the home

The host who wants to give his guests wine at home will do well to keep a small store. Although the off-licence may be just around the corner, it may be shut when the unexpected guest calls. Also, it is often cheaper: most wine-merchants will give a small discount on orders of a dozen bottles or more. Moreover, it is annoying, when another bottle of a particularly enjoyable vintage is wanted, to find that it has all been sold or that it has increased in price or that it is early-closing day.

Price increases are neither unusual nor wrong, because as wines, especially red wines, mature in bottle, they increase in quality and value. Also, each vintage has an effect on the price of its predecessors. For instance, 1966 was a good vintage for red Burgundies, while 1967 was poor, and 1968 a near-disaster. So, the 1966 Burgundies increased in value and price. This is not, by the way, to say that *all* Burgundies were good in 1966 and bad in the other two years; there is always some good wine from poor years, just as there is always some poor wine from good years. It is better to trust the judgement of a reputable wine-merchant than to go by the across-the-board statements of the vintage charts, although the best of these are useful as a rough guide. Some details of recent vintages are given in Appendix 5, but they are couched in only very general terms.

Having bought the wine, where and how should one store it? In a private house, the ideal place to keep any wines is in an unheated cellar, below ground level. Such a cellar will keep an even temperature around 9°C to 14°C (48°F to 57°F) and will also be free from vibration and light. The actual temperature, if even, is the least important of these conditions. For those who do not have a cellar, the cupboard under the stairs may be the next best place. The loft is not usually a good place for storage, because it is too hot in summer and too cold in winter.

Spirits should always be stored standing up, while wines should always be stored on their sides; keeping them on their sides will keep the corks damp, for these will lose their elasticity and ability to seal the bottle if they dry out. It is best to lay the bottles in racks, which can be obtained quite cheaply, even to fit the triangular under-stair cupboard. But, if no rack is available, the divided case in which the bottles were delivered will do as a temporary measure. The bottles should be stored with their labels uppermost, for then these can be read without undue disturbance, and also it will be known that any deposit (as in the case of older red wines) is lying on the other side of the bottle. The deposit is bitter to taste, and care should be taken when pouring to see that none gets into the glass. This can be avoided by decanting the wine from the bottle into a flask or decanter.

Serving wine

If sufficient notice has been given, it is best to take the bottle from storage to stand upright for a day before decanting, so that the sediment will fall to the bottom of the bottle. The bottle should not be disturbed when drawing the cork. The shoulders, as well as the neck of the bottle, should first be wiped so that the wine coming from the bottle can be observed. To make this easier, a light should be placed behind the bottle before decanting, so that the sediment can be seen approaching the neck. The bottle should be held label-side up, and the wine poured gently into the decanter in one steady movement, stopping when the sediment starts climbing into the neck. The half-glass of wine left in the bottle is not worth drinking, but it is a valuable asset to the cook for making sauces.

Sparkling wines should be opened with care, and the cork should never be allowed to leave the hand, lest it should hurt someone: with a pressure of up to 65 lbs per square inch, and a cork the exact size of a human eyeball, accidents could happen. The following procedure will ensure that the bottle is safely opened and that none of the precious wine is lost. Keeping the left thumb pressed firmly on the top of the bottle, release the wine muzzle which holds the cork down (the gold foil has already been removed) and lift it away. Hold the bottle at about thirty degrees from the vertical, by the base, in the right hand, protecting the hand with a napkin against the unlikely event of the bottle bursting. Still holding the cork in place firmly with the left hand, gently turn the bottle with the right. As the cork is eased out, restrained by the left hand, any surplus pressure can escape gently, allowing the wine to be poured out without loss. A discreet 'pop' may be permissible.

Obviously, the colder the sparkling wine is when opened, the lower will be the pressure and the risk of losing any wine. But although sparkling wines should be served chilled, this does *not* mean iced. Iced sparkling wine, descending into a warm stomach, explodes like a bomb, creating discomfort and embarrassment.

What are the best temperatures at which to serve wines? Fig. 36 shows the ideal temperature ranges. Sweet wines, with the notable exception of Vintage ports and Madeiras, should be

Fig. 36 165

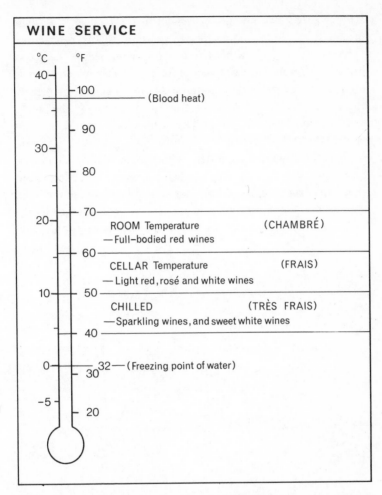

WINE SERVICE

°C °F
40
100 ———————— (Blood heat)
90
30
80
70
20
ROOM Temperature   (CHAMBRÉ)
—Full–bodied red wines
60
CELLAR Temperature   (FRAIS)
— Light red, rosé and white wines
10
50
CHILLED   (TRÈS FRAIS)
—Sparkling wines, and sweet white wines
40
0
32 —— (Freezing point of water)
30
-5
20

chilled: the sweeter, the cooler. Old Tawny port gains from
being slightly chilled. So also do light white wines. The fuller-
bodied white wines, the rosés, and the lighter red wines, are best
served at cellar temperature, while the full-bodied red wines
(that is to say, the general run of red wines) taste better if served
at room temperature.

When bringing white wines from cellar temperature to chilled temperature, care should be taken that the change is done gradually. A few minutes in the bottom of the refrigerator (*never* a freezer), or an hour in a wine-cooler, should suffice to bring a wine to the right degree of chill. The wine-cooler is often called an ice-bucket, and is sometimes misused by placing the bottle on a bed of ice which freezes the bottom of the bottle, and does not cool the wine. The wine-cooler should be deep enough to contain the whole length of the bottle, and should be half-filled with cold water: some pieces of ice should be placed in the water to keep it cool. To bring red wines from cellar up to room temperature, they should be placed in the room for several hours. Restaurants often have a 'dispense' in the dining-room, where a small supply of the more popular red

Champagne Flute   Champagne Saucer   German Wines

Sherry Sampler   Table Wines   Brandy

Fig. 37   *Glass Shapes*

wines are kept. But, if a bottle has to be brought directly from the cellar, it should *never* be placed in the oven or in hot water: such treatment would harm the bouquet. The only artificial method that might be acceptable is to decant the wine into a warmed (not hot) decanter, but it is really better to tell the guests that the wine should be warmed in the glass with the hand, and to serve a lesser quantity in the glass until the wine has had time to come to room temperature.

Particularly if this method of warming the wine is necessary, the glass should be thin; it should also be large enough to contain a reasonable amount of wine when filled two thirds full – the proper level. It should be of clear glass, so that the consumer can see the colour of the wine, and it should be tulip-shaped, to conserve the aroma for the nose. Glasses for white wine should have a long stem, so that the hand does not warm the wine, nor the wine chill the hand. Fig. 37 shows five shapes of glass generally encountered. Note that the saucer-shaped glass is unsuitable for sparkling wines, as it lets the bubbles escape too quickly.

This elementary study of alcoholic drinks and their industries is intended to provide an introduction for the uninitiated, and it is hoped that two things have been achieved. Firstly, that it will have encouraged the reader to learn more (Appendix 6 lists a few of the many books available), and secondly, that it will have brought a greater appreciation of wines, spirits and beers, and through that, a greater enjoyment of them.

Appendix 1   Vine varieties

The following chart, called an ampelograph, is intended as a guide
only to the principal types of grape grown in different countries,
regions and districts, and to the types of wine made from them. For
reasons of space, it is not exhaustive; it is, for instance, only possible
to show the principal types of wine made from each grape – although
often red, white and rosé wines may be made from the same grape.
Many grape types have had to be omitted, and the selection has not
been easy.

   The chart is also a simplification: many may say, an over-simpli-
fication. The Ugni Blanc is not *exactly* the same grape as the Treb-
biano, any more than Jolyon Forsyte was the same as Soames – but
they are closely enough related to be grouped together. Even in
Champagne, the Pinot Noir shows slight variations from village to
village. Nor has account been taken of the fact that some grapes,
notably the Grenache and the Malvasia, exist in both black and white
form; in such cases, the black form has been quoted to avoid the
anomaly of making red or rosé wine from white grapes. It must also
be noted that several grapes shown as white, in particular the Gewürztraminer, have lightly-coloured skins; but to call them rosé would
invite confusion.

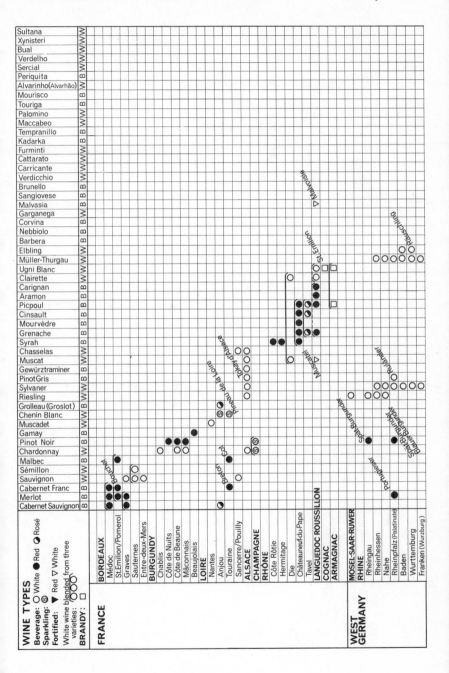

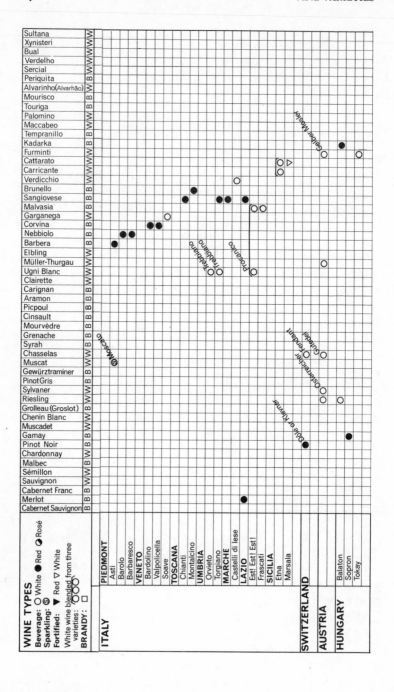

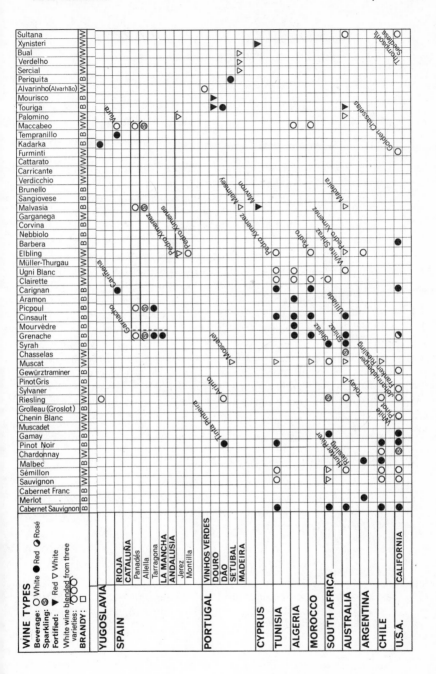

Appendix 2   Pests and diseases

Parasites

Phylloxera Vastatrix

A burrowing vine louse native to America. This tiny insect was first observed in 1863 in a greenhouse at Hammersmith. *Phylloxera* is an aphid fly with a phenomenal rate of reproduction. During its remarkable life cycle (which has nineteen stages), it attacks the root cells, the cane and the leaf of the vine, and completely destroys it. In the final form of the cycle, the winged insect can fly down-wind for as much as 30 miles, where its progeny, after mating, regenerate the life cycle. France was first affected in 1863, and by 1870 the insect had been identified in Bordeaux, Portugal and the Rhône Valley. Over the following 25 years it spread ruthlessly through the Palatinate, Burgundy, Italy, Algeria, South Africa, Champagne and Jerez in Spain. By the end of the century most European vineyards had been uprooted, producing an acute shortage of wine. The pest cannot be eradicated, and vines must be uprooted, burned, and the soil sterilized with carbon disulphide in order to clean a vineyard. At the present time, vines throughout the world are grown on North American root-stocks, except in Chile and a few isolated districts elsewhere.

Eel Worms *(Nematodes)*

These threadlike worms puncture the root of the vine and form calluses. They attack the same kinds of root-stock as *Phylloxera*, and the treatment is the same. Eel worms are in fact second only to *Phylloxera* as an enemy of the vine.

Meal Moth *(Pyralis)*

The caterpillar of the meal moth will eat the emergent shoots of the vine. It is controlled with insecticides, including arsenic- and nicotine-based sprays.

Grape-berry moths *(Cochylis* and *Eudemis)*

The caterpillars feed on the young grape blossom and on the newly-formed fruit. Treatment as for Meal Moth.

Altise

This beetle feeds on the leaves of the vine. Treatment as for Meal Moth.

Cockchafers or May Bugs *(Melolontha Vulgaris)*

The fat white grubs of the cockchafer gnaw at the surface roots of the vine. Treatment as for Meal Moth.

General

Other parasites include wasps, birds and weeds, against each of which conventional treatments are used.

Fungal Diseases (Cryptogams)

Powdery Mildew *(Oïdium Tuckeri)*

Native to the USA, and first observed in Kew gardens in 1850. It went on to attack the vines of Madeira and sweep through Europe. *Oïdium* lodges in dormant shoots, affecting the new growth and eventually the grapes, covering them with a white deposit; the grapes split, rot and dry up. *Oïdium* is treated with sulphur spray before and after blossoming, and by dusting with flowers of sulphur.

Downy Mildew *(Peronospera)*

Peronospera reached Europe via South Africa from the USA in 1878. It appears under conditions of high humidity, and affects the leaves of the vine. It also attacks the grapes, which shrivel, rot and dry up. Oily transparent patches appear on the leaf as a danger signal. The airborne spores are activated by rain or dew and pass into the young leaves, repeated in a two-week cycle. Copper- and zinc-based sprays are effective and must be applied in each cycle. Dead leaves should be cleared from the vineyard, as these carry the disease.

Black Rot

This fungus from the USA appears as black spots on the leaves of the vine, and shrivels the fruit. It occurs in warm, humid conditions. The treatment is as for Downy Mildew.

Anthracnose

This disease, of European origin, develops in the same conditions as Black Rot, and the treatment is the same. Stains appear on the leaf and on the grape, turning into holes.

Grey Rot, or Pourriture Grise *(Botrytis Cinerea)*

In warm damp weather, this fungus attacks the leaves and fruit of the vine – particularly those which have already been attacked by other diseases – causing alterations within the grapes and imparting an unpleasant flavour to the wine. It is recognized by a grey mould, and can be controlled by standard methods of vineyard hygiene.

Noble Rot, or Pourriture Noble

This is the same fungus in its beneficent form, which may occur when humid conditions are followed by hot weather. In these conditions, the filaments of the fungus puncture the grape skin, extracting water for its nourishment. In the process, the grape shrivels and turns golden brown, concentrating the sugar inside; the fungus converts some sugar to glycerine, giving the luscious flavour to the wine characteristic of Sauternes, German *Trockenbeerenausleses* and Hungarian Tokay.

Virus

Fan Leaf *(Court Noué)*

This virus causes a degeneration of the vine, and grafted vines are non-resistant. The leaf turns yellow and becomes misshapen, and the shoots grow laterally. The treatment is to grub up the vines and disinfect the vineyard.

Physiological Disorders

Chlorosis

Excessive chalk in the soil may prevent some vines from assimilating iron, resulting in a lack of chlorophyll. The condition can be treated with ferrous sulphate, but prevention lies in the choice of vine variety.

Coulure

Bad weather during the flowering season may result in poor pollination, yielding sparse bunches of grapes. Later, some of the berries may fail to develop, remaining small, green and hard. This condition is known as *millerandage*.

Appendix 3   Official classifications of Bordeaux and Burgundy wines

Bordeaux

This classification has been widely disputed, and one change has already been made; it is usually more important for the reader to remember which growth a particular château falls into, than its exact position in the list. To facilitate reference, we have therefore departed from the original order (which may be found in most books on Bordeaux wines), and have arranged châteaux in alphabetical order for each growth, with the exception of the First Great Growths.

Most names in Bordeaux are prefixed by the term Château, but where a different term such as *Clos* is used, this is shown in italics.

The 1855 official classification of the wines of the Gironde

Red wines

Premiers Crus	Château	Appellation Contrôlée
Premiers Crus	Ch. Lafite	*Pauillac*
	Ch. Latour	*Pauillac*
	Ch. Margaux	*Margaux*
	Ch. Haut-Brion	*Graves*
	Ch. Mouton-Rothschild (elevated to Premier Cru by Presidential decree 1973)	*Pauillac*
Seconds Crus	Ch. Brane-Cantenac	*Margaux*
	Ch. Cos d'Estournel	*St. Estèphe*
	Ch. Ducru-Beaucaillou	*St. Julien*
	Ch. Durfort-Vivens	*Margaux*
	Ch. Gruaud-Larose	*St. Julien*

	Ch. Lascombes	*Margaux*
	Ch. Léoville-Barton	*St. Julien*
	Ch. Léoville-Las-Cases	*St. Julien*
	Ch. Léoville-Poyferré	*St. Julien*
	Ch. Montrose	*St. Estèphe*
	Ch. Pichon-Longueville	*Pauillac*
	Ch. Pichon-Longueville-Lalande	*Pauillac*
	Ch. Rauzan-Gassies	*Margaux*
	Ch. Rausan-Ségla	*Margaux*
Troisièmes Crus	Ch. Boyd-Cantenac	*Margaux*
	Ch. Calon-Ségur	*St. Estèphe*
	Ch. Cantenac-Brown	*Margaux*
	Ch. Desmirail	*Margaux*
	Ch. Ferrière	*Margaux*
	Ch. Giscours	*Margaux*
	Ch. d'Issan	*Margaux*
	Ch. Kirwan	*Margaux*
	Ch. Lagrange	*St. Julien*
	Ch. Langoa	*St. Julien*
	Ch. La Lagune	*Haut-Médoc*
	Ch. Malescot-St-Exupéry	*Margaux*
	Ch. Marquis d'Alesme-Becker	*Margaux*
	Ch. Palmer	*Margaux*
Quatrièmes Crus	Ch. Beychevelle	*St. Julien*
	Ch. Branaire-Ducru	*St. Julien*
	Ch. Duhart-Milon	*Pauillac*
	Ch. Lafon-Rochet	*St. Estèphe*
	Ch. La Tour-Carnet	*Haut-Médoc*
	Ch. Marquis-de-Terme	*Margaux*
	Ch. Pouget	*Margaux*
	Ch. Prieuré-Lichine	*Margaux*
	Ch. St-Pierre-Bontemps	*St. Julien*
	Ch. St-Pierre-Sevaistre	*St. Julien*
	Ch. Talbot	*St. Julien*
Cinquièmes Crus	Ch. Batailley	*Pauillac*
	Ch. Belgrave	*Haut-Médoc*
	Ch. Camensac	*Haut-Médoc*
	Ch. Cantemerle	*Haut-Médoc*

Ch. Clerc-Milon-Mondon	*Pauillac*
Ch. Cos Labory	*St. Estèphe*
Ch. Croizet-Bages	*Pauillac*
Ch. Dauzac	*Margaux*
Ch. du Tertre	*Margaux*
Ch. Grand-Puy-Ducasse	*Pauillac*
Ch. Grand-Puy-Lacoste	*Pauillac*
Ch. Haut-Bages-Libéral	*Pauillac*
Ch. Haut-Batailley	*Pauillac*
Ch. Lynch-Bages	*Pauillac*
Ch. Lynch-Moussas	*Pauillac*
Ch. Mouton-Baron-Philippe	*Pauillac*
Ch. Pédesclaux	*Pauillac*
Ch. Pontet-Canet	*Pauillac*

White wines

Premier Grand Cru	Ch. d'Yquem	*Sauternes*
Premiers Crus	Ch. Climens	*Barsac & Sauternes*
	Ch. Coutet	*Barsac & Sauternes*
	Ch. de Rayne-Vigneau	*Sauternes*
	Ch. de Suduiraut	*Sauternes*
	Ch. Guiraud	*Sauternes*
	Clos Haut-Peyraguey	*Sauternes*
	Ch. Lafaurie-Peyraguey	*Sauternes*
	Ch. La Tour-Blanche	*Sauternes*
	Ch. Rabaud-Promis	*Sauternes*
	Ch. Rieussec	*Sauternes*
	Ch. Sigalas-Rabaud	*Sauternes*
Seconds Crus	Ch. Broustet	*Barsac & Sauternes*
	Ch. Caillou	*Barsac & Sauternes*
	Ch. d'Arche	*Sauternes*
	Ch. de Malle	*Sauternes*
	Ch. de Myrat	*Barsac & Sauternes*
	Ch. Doisy-Daëne	*Barsac & Sauternes*
	Ch. Doisy-Védrines	*Barsac & Sauternes*
	Ch. Filhot	*Sauternes*
	Ch. Lamothe	*Sauternes*

Ch. Nairac — *Barsac & Sauternes*
Ch. Romer — *Sauternes*
Ch. Suau — *Barsac & Sauternes*

St. Emilion 1955 official classification

Appellation St. Emilion Premier Grand Cru Classé A Contrôlée	Ch. Ausone Ch. Cheval Blanc
Appellation St. Emilion Premier Grand Cru Classé B Contrôlée	Ch. Beauséjour Ch. Belair Ch. Canon Ch. Figeac *Clos* Fourtet Ch. La Gaffelière Ch. Magdelaine Ch. Pavie Ch. Trottevieille
Appellation St. Emilion Grand Cru Classé Contrôlée	Ch. l'Angélus Ch. l'Arrosée Ch. Baleau Ch. Balestard-la-Tonnelle Ch. Bellevue Ch. Bergat Ch. Cadet-Bon Ch. Cadet-Piola Ch. Canon-La Gaffelière Ch. Cap-de-Mourlin Ch. Chapelle-Madeleine Ch. Chauvin Ch. Corbin Ch. Corbin-Michotte Ch. Coutet *Couvent* des Jacobins Ch. Curé Bon Ch. Dassault *Clos* des Jacobins Ch. Fonplégade Ch. Fonroque

Ch. Franc-Mayne
Ch. Grand-Barrail-Lamarzelle-Figeac
Ch. Grand-Corbin Despagne
Ch. Grand-Corbin-Pécresse
Ch. Grand-Mayne
Ch. Grand-Pontet
Ch. Grandes-Murailles
Ch. Guadet-St-Julien
Ch. Haut Corbin
Ch. Haut Sarpe
Ch. Jean-Faure
Ch. La Carte
Ch. La Clotte
Ch. La Cluzière
Ch. La Couspade
Ch. La Dominique
Clos La Madeleine
Ch. Larcis-Ducasse
Ch. Lamarzelle
Ch. Lamiote
Ch. Larmande
Ch. Laroze
Ch. Lasserre
Ch. La-Tour-Figeac
Ch. La-Tour-du-Pin-Figeac
Ch. Le Châtelet
Ch. Le Couvent
Ch. Le Prieuré
Ch. Matras
Ch. Mauvezin
Ch. Moulin-du-Cadet
Clos de l'Oratoire
Ch. Pavie-Decesse
Ch. Pavie-Macquin
Ch. Pavillon-Cadet
Ch. Petit-Faurie-de-Souchard
Ch. Petit-Faurie-de-Soutard
Ch. Ripeau
Ch. Sansonnet
Ch. St-Georges-Côte-Pavie

Clos St-Martin
Ch. Soutard
Ch. Tertre-Daugay
Ch. Trimoulet
Ch. Trois Moulins
Ch. Troplong-Mondot
Ch. Villemaurine
Ch. Yon-Figeac

Graves 1959 official classification

Red wines

Appellation Graves Contrôlée

Ch. Bouscaut
Ch. Carbonnieux
Domaine de Chevalier
Ch. Fieuzal
Ch. Haut-Bailly
Ch. Haut-Brion
Ch. La Mission-Haut-Brion
Ch. La Tour-Haut-Brion
Ch. La Tour-Martillac
Ch. Malartic-Lagravière
Ch. Olivier
Ch. Pape-Clément
Ch. Smith-Haut-Lafitte

White wines

Appellation Graves Contrôlée

Ch. Bouscaut
Ch. Carbonnieux
Domaine de Chevalier
Ch. Couhins
Ch. La Tour-Martillac
Ch. Laville-Haut-Brion
Ch. Marlatic-Lagravière
Ch. Olivier

Burgundy

Appellations Grands Crus
Contrôlées, Côte de Nuits

Gevrey-Chambertin
Chambertin
Chambertin-Clos-de-Bèze
Chapelle-Chambertin
Charmes-Chambertin
Griotte-Chambertin
Latricières-Chambertin
Mazis-Chambertin
Mazoyères-Chambertin
Ruchottes-Chambertin
Morey-St-Denis
Bonnes-Mares (also in Chambolle-Musigny)
Clos-de-la-Roche
Clos-de-Tart (also in Chambolle-Musigny)
Clos-St-Denis
Chambolle-Musigny
Bonnes-Mares (also in Morey-St-Denis)
Clos-de-Tart (also in Morey-St-Denis)
Musigny (including a little white wine)
Vougeot
Clos-de-Vougeot
Vosne-Romanée
Echézeaux
Grands-Echézeaux
La Tâche
Richebourg
Romanée-Conti
Romanée-St-Vivant

Côte de Beaune

Aloxe-Corton
Charlemagne (white wines only, but no wine under this *appellation* has been marketed for some time)

Corton (red wine and some
white)
Corton-Charlemagne (white
wine only)
Puligny-Montrachet & *Chassagne-
Montrachet* (white wines only)
Bâtard-Montrachet
Bienvenues-Bâtard-Montrachet
Chevalier-Montrachet
Criots-Bâtard-Montrachet
Montrachet

Appendix 4   Mixed drinks

The mixing of drinks is an ancient art – the Greeks and Romans used to mix herbs and spices with their drinks at table. In these days, mixed drinks fall into several categories: punches, hot and cold; wine cups; *apéritifs*; cocktails; and pick-me-ups.

For punches and cups, the advice given by Colonel Peter Hawker in his *Hints to Young Shooters* published in 1844, is still the best:

'Here is a recipe in the form of a rhyme which any shallow-headed boy may readily remember:

> One sour
> Two sweet
> Four strong
> Eight weak

But for cold punches, which may by their refreshing nature beguile the consumer, *twenty* weak should be substituted.'

Translated into a detailed recipe for hot punch, this would give:

One sour – the juice of one lemon

Two sweet – double the sour quantity of sugar or honey

Four strong – double the sweet quantity of spirit – say rum, whisky, whiskey or brandy

Eight weak – double the strong quantity of wine, beer, cider or even water

Heat all the ingredients *except the spirit* with spices (usually ginger, cinnamon, nutmeg or allspice as desired) to near boiling-point, but do not boil. Add the spirit and serve in heat-proof glasses. A rum punch is improved if a little brandy is included, and also if a small pat of butter is added to the hot mixture before the spirit.

There is a large permutation of ingredients which may be used, and the results are often given special names: for instance Bishop (port and Burgundy), Pope (port and brandy), Glühwein (hard red wine and brandy), and Wassail (Marsala and brandy with the addition of eggs).

For the occasion when a lot of cold wet friends arrive on the doorstep, here is a recipe for quick punch:

Heat three bottles of red wine with one bottle of ginger wine and the juice of two lemons, together with a stick of cinnamon. Add a quarter bottle of brandy and serve. (Five minutes, for thirty glasses).

Cold punches and cups should always be well chilled. Claret or cider cup can be pre-mixed to serve a large number of people, but there are many other long drinks which are usually mixed individually. The following are some examples:

Planters' Punch   Fresh lime, rum and soda.

The Collins's   Fresh lemon or lime, gin and soda. 'John' uses Dutch or London gin; 'Tom' uses sweetened Old Tom gin.

Horse's Neck   Gin or whisky, ice and ginger ale.

Dog's Nose   Gin and ginger beer; this is a little dog. Gin and light ale; this is a big dog. Which is taken may depend upon the size of the one encountered the night before.

Sangria   Sweetened orange juice and red wine.

Shandygaffs   Usually known as shandy. These consist of a half-and-half mixture of bitter beer and either ginger beer or lemonade. 'Lager and Lime' is a modern variation and consists of putting a small quantity of concentrated lime juice into lager.

Redeye   Half tomato juice, half bitter beer. An acquired taste, beloved by French Canadians.

Black Velvet   Half chilled Champagne, half Guinness.

Bucks' Fizz   Half chilled Champagne, half orange juice, served in a large goblet with a dash of brandy.

Buck's Head   One part Spanish brandy to three parts fresh orange juice.

Champagne Cocktail   Put a lump of sugar in the bottom of a goblet and shake three drops of angostura bitters on to it; add a measure of brandy and a dash of curaçao. Fill with chilled Champagne. Replenish with straight Champagne.

This marks the division between the long drink, which may be taken at any time of day, and the *apéritif* or cocktail, taken to sharpen the appetite before a meal. There are thousands of different cocktail recipes; the following are a few of those most likely to be encountered:

Gin and French   Half gin, half dry French vermouth.

Martini   Two parts dry London gin to one part of dry French vermouth.

Dry Martini   Dry London gin with a dash of dry French vermouth.

Bronx   Two parts gin to one part each of sweet Italian vermouth and dry French vermouth, with a dash of orange bitters and a tablespoonful of orange juice.

White Lady   Two parts dry gin to one part each of Cointreau and fresh lemon juice.

Pink Gin   Put three or four drops of angostura bitters in a glass and swirl them round; some like the bitters left in, others like it shaken out. Add gin and water to taste.

Many cocktails are improved by a drop of angostura bitters, which serves to sharpen the flavour of the various ingredients. This is especially true of the Gimlet.

Gimlet   Half gin, half concentrated lime juice.

Screwdriver   Two parts of vodka to one part of orange juice with a half teaspoonful of caster sugar.

Bloody Mary   Three parts tomato juice to one part vodka, with a teaspoonful of Worcester sauce and the same quantity of lemon juice; add a shake of red pepper and celery salt.

Manhattan   Two parts rye or bourbon whiskey to one part each of dry French vermouth and sweet Italian vermouth. This is the whiskey counterpart of its New York neighbour, the Bronx.

Americano   Two parts of sweet Italian vermouth to one part of Campari.

Sidecar   Two parts brandy to one part each of Cointreau and fresh lemon juice. This is the brandy counterpart of the White Lady.

It cannot be too strongly emphasized that all these cocktails must be *very* well chilled.

Old Fashioned   Rub a lump of sugar on the rind of an orange. Place it in the bottom of a tumbler with a slice of orange, and crush the two together with a pestle. Fill the tumbler to the brim with crushed ice. Then fill up the gaps in the ice with bourbon whiskey.

Mint Julep   In a tall tumbler place alternate layers of *crushed* ice and shredded mint leaves until the tumbler is full. Fill up the gaps in the ice with bourbon whiskey.

The Old Fashioned and the Mint Julep are replenished by adding bourbon whiskey until the glass is full again, which means that the drink gets stronger and stronger as the nose gets colder. The Mint Julep is less of a cocktail than a way of life.

It is not usual to serve mixed drinks after dinner, but two deserve mention.

Irish Coffee   In a large goblet put two tablespoonfuls of brown sugar and fill threequarters full with black coffee; stir well. Add Irish whiskey, and immediately float thick cream over the back of a spoon on to the surface, covering the whole. Those mistaking this for Guinness will burn themselves. Variations using brandy or Scotch whisky are called by appropriate names.

Pousse-café   An old Victorian seduction trick which consisted of pouring coloured liqueurs of different specific gravities into a special-shaped glass, and inviting the admiring young lady to drink the multi-coloured result. This 'Pousse-café' is very pretty to look at, and rather alcoholic. The order is as follows: Crème de Cacao; Blue Curaçao; Yellow Chartreuse; Maraschino; Benedictine; Green Chartreuse; Cognac.

On occasions when the 'morning after' is tiresome, the following recipes may help to redress the situation:

Prairie Oysters   These are for the really unwell, and here are two of several variations:

Oyster 1   One ounce of cognac and one teaspoonful each of wine vinegar and Worcester sauce; add a dash of red pepper. Pour this mixture over a whole raw egg and drink without breaking the yolk.

Oyster 2   To a can of tomato juice add four dashes of angostura bitters and a dash of Worcester sauce. Float a whole raw egg on top and help the afflicted to drink it, before it looks at him.

Bullshot   Stir two ounces of vodka and a teaspoonful of Worcester sauce, with the juice of half a lemon and a dash of red pepper, into a can of chilled condensed consommé.

Port and Brandy   This has no name, but is very soothing to the stomach.

Appendix 5   Some recent Vintages

Red Bordeaux

Poor	Average	Excellent	Poor	Average	Excellent
		1945		1960	
1946					1961
	1947				1962
	1948		1963		
		1949		1964	
	1950		1965		
1951					1966
	1952				1967
	1953		1968		
1954				1969	
	1955				1970
1956				1971	
	1957			1972?*	
	1958			1973?	
		1959			

Sauternes

Poor	Average	Excellent	Poor	Average	Excellent
		1950			1962
1951			1963		
	1952		1964		
		1953	1965		
1954				1966	
		1955		1967	
1956			1968		
	1957			1969	
	1958				1970
		1959			1971
1960				1972	
		1961			1973?

*Note: Where a question mark follows the date, this indicates that it is as yet too early to be certain of the grading; however the probability has been calculated.

Red Burgundy

Poor	Average	Excellent	Poor	Average	Excellent
1956	1955		1965		1966
	1957			1967	
1958			1968		
		1959			1969
1960				1970	
	1961				1971
	1962				1972?
1963				1973?	
		1964			

White Burgundy

Poor	Average	Excellent	Poor	Average	Excellent
1960			1968		1967
	1961				
		1962			1969
1963					1970
		1964			1971
1965					1972?
		1966		1973?	

Rhine and Moselle

Poor	Average	Excellent	Poor	Average	Excellent
		1964			1969
1965				1970	
	1966				1971
	1967		1972		
1968				1973?	

Champagne – Generally declared Vintages

1961	1964	1969?
1962	1966	1970?

Port – Generally declared Vintages

1945	1954	1963
1947	1955	1966
1948	1958	1967
1950	1960	1970

Appendix 6   A short bibliography

Let's Talk about Port by Valente Perfeito — Instituto do Vinho do Porto, 1948

Sherry by Manuel M. Gonzalez Gordon — Cassell and Company Ltd, 1948*

Madeira by Croft Cooke — Putnam and Company, 1961

A History of Wine by H. Warner Allen — Faber and Faber, 1961

The Science and Technique of Wine by Lionel Frumkin — H. C. Lea and Company Ltd, 1964

A History of English Ale and Beer by H. A. Monckton — The Bodley Head, 1966

Wine by Hugh Johnson — Thomas Nelson and Sons Ltd, 1966

An Encyclopaedia of Wines and Spirits by Alexis Lichine — Cassell, 1967

Champagne by Patrick Forbes — Victor Gollancz Ltd, 1967

Liqueurs by Peter Hallgarten — Wine and Spirit Publications Ltd, 1967

Teach Yourself Wine by R. S. Don, MW — The English Universities Press Ltd, 1968

Applied Wine Chemistry and Technology by A. Massel — Heidelberg Publishers Ltd, 1969

Plain Guide to Licensing Law — Brewing Publications Ltd, 1969

Learning about Wines and Spirits — Wine and Spirit Education Trust Ltd, 1970

World Atlas of Wine by Hugh Johnson — Maison Fondee-Mitchell Beazley, 1971

Vendange by Andrew Durkan — Edward Arnold, 1971

The Wines of Italy by Cyril Ray — Penguin Books, 1971

The Great Wine Blight by George Ordish — J. M. Dent and Sons Ltd, 1972

Innkeeping by J. G. Miles, FITO (Editor) — Barrie and Jenkins (for the National Trade Development Association), 1972

Eating and Drinking in France Today by Pamela Vandyke Price — Tom Stacey, 1972

*Revised edition, Wine and Spirit Publications Ltd, 1972

Eating with Wine by Guirne Van Zuylen — Faber and Faber, 1972

The Compact Wine Guide by Luke Bayard — Wine and Spirit Publications Ltd, 1973

Wines and Spirits by L. W. Marrison — Penguin Books, 1973

The Beer Drinker's Companion by Frank Baillie — David and Charles, 1973

Wine Tasting by J. M. Broadbent, MW — Christie Wine Publications, 1973

Behind the Label by Tim Holland — Bass Charrington Vintners, 1974

he nose
orzhwah,

Chassagne-Montrachet,
  shassine-mawnrashay
Chasselas, *shassuhlah*
Château, *shato*, literally *castle*,
  applied to a French mansion
  and to its vineyard.
  Abbreviated to 'Ch.' See also
  'Domaine'

w)
gallons
, and
s

Châteauneuf-du-Pape,
  shatohnuf-doo-pap
Chenin Blanc, *shenan blaw*
Chianti, *keeanti*
Chinon, *sheenaw*
Cinsault, *sansoh*
Classico, **klas**seekoh
Climens (Ch.), *kleemaw*

ay

burnay-

Coaster, a tray, sometimes on
  wheels, for holding a decanter
  or bottle, to be passed round
  a dining-table

le kakow
ng-

ly thin
of a
which
n the
aft to

Cognac, *konyak*
Cointreau, *kwahntroh*
Condrieu, *kondree-uh*
Corky, a rotten, persistent
  smell, caused by a cork that
  has gone bad
Côte d'Or, *koht dor*
Coutet (Ch.), *kootay*
Criadera, *kreeadairuh*
Curaçao, *kyoorasoh*

ard
d
ottles,
nums,

ottles
d
m

Deidesheim, *die-des-hime*
Doisy-Daëne, *dwahzee-den*
Domaine, the
  Burgundian equivalent of a
  château
Dordogne, *dordoyn*
Doux, *doo*

bol-

Ducru-Beaucaillou (Ch.),
  dookroo-bohke ye-yoo
d'Yquem (Ch.), *deekem*

Appendix 7   The metric system, with useful conversions

The British wine trade is already geared to the metric system and has, for several years, used metric measures, particularly for bottle sizes. Some conversions, and the correct method of writing the metric symbols, are given in this Appendix. In this connection, it should be noted carefully that 'litres' should always be spelled out in full to avoid confusion, as the lower case letter 'l' is often used to denote the figure 1.

There is no need for an overnight adoption of the metric system, such as happened with currency decimalization. A less dramatic and gradual approach is more appropriate for this field, which encompasses all dimensions. Already centigrade is mentioned more than fahrenheit; hectolitres per hectare are mentioned more than gallons per acre; degrees Gay-Lussac more than Sikes; centilitres more than fluid ounces and cubic centimetres or millilitres more than fractions of a gill.

The mind of man does not change in an instant, nor can it be coerced into doing so. Succeeding generations will learn only the new terms; the present generation will gradually learn to convert; and, in time, the old measures will pass into the web of history, to join the league and the ell.

Metric Scales

Basic Units

Length: 1 metre $= 3 \cdot 28$ feet
Area: 1 are $= 119 \cdot 6$ square yards
Weight: 1 gram $= 0 \cdot 03$ ounces
          1 Tonne $= 0 \cdot 984$ tons
Volume
Capacity: 1 litre $= 61 \cdot 03$ cubic inches $= 1 \cdot 76$ pints

Multiple and Sub-Multiple Prefixes

Ten	Deca-	Decametre (Dm)
One hundred	Hecto-	Hectolitre (Hl)
One thousand	Kilo-	Kilogram (Kg)
One million	Mega-	MegaTonne (MT)
One thousand million	Giga-	GigaHerz (GHz)
One million million	Tera-	

One tenth	deci-	decilitre (dl)
One hundredth	centi-	centimetre (cm)
One thousandth	milli-	millilitre (ml)
One millionth	micro-	microgram (µg)
One thousand millionth	nano-	nanosecond (ns)
One million millionth	pica-	picometre (pm)

Approximate Equivalents

1 inch = 25 millimetres (mm)

13 feet = 4 metres (m)

22 yards = 20 metres

5 miles = 8 kilometres (Km)

3 square inches = 20 square centimetres (cm^2)

$2\frac{1}{2}$ acres = 1 Hectare (Ha)

4 cubic inches = 65 cubic centimetres (cc) = 65 millilitres (ml)

3 cubic feet = 85 litres = 0·085 cubic metres (m^3)

1 gallon = 4·5 litres

$1\frac{3}{4}$ pints = 1 litre (= 7 gills = 35 fluid ounces)

$26\frac{2}{3}$ fluid ounces = 75 centilitres (cl)

22 gallons = 1 Hectolitre (Hl)

$\frac{1}{6}$ gill = 2 centilitres

$\frac{1}{5}$ gill = 2·75 centilitres

1 ton = 1016 Kilograms (Kg) = 1·016 Tonnes (T)

22 pounds = 10 Kilograms

1 pound = 540 grams (g)

3 ounces = 85 grams

300 gallons per acre = 34 Hectolitres per Hectare (Hl/Ha)

1 ton per acre = 2·5 Tonnes per Hectare (T/Ha)

15 pounds per acre = 17 Kilograms per Hectare (Kg/Ha)

1 pound per gallon = 100 grams per litre (gm/litre)

1 part per million (ppm) = 1 milligram per litre (mg/litre)

$38\frac{1}{2}$ proof gallons = 1 Hectolitre of pure (100°GL) alcohol

Glo

Abboccato,
term mea
Acetic, ta
Acetobacte
bacteriu
which c
alcohol
acid (vi
Acid, a
wine to
sweetn
import
wine w
and it
apples
Advocaa
Albariza
Aloxe-C
Alsace,
Alvarhã
Alvarin
Amont
Añada,
Anjou,
Aramc
Armag
Arom:
disc
Artisa
wit
rar
of
Gr
E
Astr
pr
p:
to
t:

wine discovered by
Bourgeois Growths, b
see Artisan Growths
Bourgueil, *boorguh-ee*
Brouillis, *brooyee*
Brut, *broo*
Bual, *booal*
Butt, a Spanish cask
(particularly of sherr
containing about 108
(just under 500 litres
yielding 51 to 53 case

Cabernet Franc, *kaburn
fraw*
Cabernet-Sauvignon, *ka
sohveenyaw*
Cacao, Crème de, *krem*
Calon-Ségur (Ch.) *kalah
saygoor*
Cambium, the extreme
layer beneath the bark
twig, branch or trunk,
must be joined betwee
stock and scion for a g
succeed
Carignan, *kareenyaw*
Carton, Case, the stand
selling unit of wines an
spirits, containing 12 b
24 half bottles or 6 mag
amounting to 9 litres.
A carton of Bordeaux b
weighs 22 kg (48 lbs) an
measures 26 × 39 × 33 c
(10″ × 15″ × 13″)
Chablis, *shablee*
Chai, *shay*
Chambolle-Musigny, *shom
moozeeny*
Chardonnay, *shardonay*

Appendix 7 The metric system, with useful conversions

The British wine trade is already geared to the metric system and has, for several years, used metric measures, particularly for bottle sizes. Some conversions, and the correct method of writing the metric symbols, are given in this Appendix. In this connection, it should be noted carefully that 'litres' should always be spelled out in full to avoid confusion, as the lower case letter 'l' is often used to denote the figure 1.

There is no need for an overnight adoption of the metric system, such as happened with currency decimalization. A less dramatic and gradual approach is more appropriate for this field, which encompasses all dimensions. Already centigrade is mentioned more than fahrenheit; hectolitres per hectare are mentioned more than gallons per acre; degrees Gay-Lussac more than Sikes; centilitres more than fluid ounces and cubic centimetres or millilitres more than fractions of a gill.

The mind of man does not change in an instant, nor can it be coerced into doing so. Succeeding generations will learn only the new terms; the present generation will gradually learn to convert; and, in time, the old measures will pass into the web of history, to join the league and the ell.

Metric Scales

Basic Units

Length: 1 metre $= 3 \cdot 28$ feet
Area: 1 are $= 119 \cdot 6$ square yards
Weight: 1 gram $= 0 \cdot 03$ ounces
          1 Tonne $= 0 \cdot 984$ tons
Volume
Capacity: 1 litre $= 61 \cdot 03$ cubic inches $= 1 \cdot 76$ pints

Multiple and Sub-Multiple Prefixes

Ten	Deca–	Decametre (Dm)
One hundred	Hecto–	Hectolitre (Hl)
One thousand	Kilo–	Kilogram (Kg)
One million	Mega–	MegaTonne (MT)
One thousand million	Giga–	GigaHerz (GHz)
One million million	Tera–	

One tenth	deci-	decilitre (dl)
One hundredth	centi-	centimetre (cm)
One thousandth	milli-	millilitre (ml)
One millionth	micro-	microgram (µg)
One thousand millionth	nano-	nanosecond (ns)
One million millionth	pica-	picometre (pm)

Approximate Equivalents

1 inch = 25 millimetres (mm)

13 feet = 4 metres (m)

22 yards = 20 metres

5 miles = 8 kilometres (Km)

3 square inches = 20 square centimetres (cm^2)

$2\frac{1}{2}$ acres = 1 Hectare (Ha)

4 cubic inches = 65 cubic centimetres (cc) = 65 millilitres (ml)

3 cubic feet = 85 litres = $0 \cdot 085$ cubic metres (m^3)

1 gallon = $4 \cdot 5$ litres

$1\frac{3}{4}$ pints = 1 litre (= 7 gills = 35 fluid ounces)

$26\frac{2}{3}$ fluid ounces = 75 centilitres (cl)

22 gallons = 1 Hectolitre (Hl)

$\frac{1}{6}$ gill = 2 centilitres

$\frac{1}{5}$ gill = $2 \cdot 75$ centilitres

1 ton = 1016 Kilograms (Kg) = $1 \cdot 016$ Tonnes (T)

22 pounds = 10 Kilograms

1 pound = 540 grams (g)

3 ounces = 85 grams

300 gallons per acre = 34 Hectolitres per Hectare (Hl/Ha)

1 ton per acre = $2 \cdot 5$ Tonnes per Hectare (T/Ha)

15 pounds per acre = 17 Kilograms per Hectare (Kg/Ha)

1 pound per gallon = 100 grams per litre (gm/litre)

1 part per million (ppm) = 1 milligram per litre (mg/litre)

$38\frac{1}{2}$ proof gallons = 1 Hectolitre of pure (100°GL) alcohol

Glossary and pronunciation guide

Abboccato, *abo***kah***toh*,   Italian term meaning sweet

Acetic,   tasting of vinegar

Acetobacter, *asseetohbakter*,   a bacterium containing enzymes which convert the ethyl alcohol of wine into acetic acid (vinegar)

Acid,   a desirable constituent of wine to balance alcohol and sweetness. The amount is important: too little and the wine will be flat; too much and it will be tart like green apples

Advocaat, *advohkah*

Albariza, *alba***ree***thuh*

Aloxe-Corton, *aloss-kortaw*

Alsace, *alsass*

Alvarhão, *alvaruhn*

Alvarinho, *alva***reen***yoo*

Amontillado, *amontee***yah***doh*

Añada, *an***yah***dah*

Anjou, *awnzhoo*

Aramon, *aramaw*

Armagnac, *armanyak*

Aroma,   the taste of wine discovered in the mouth

Artisan Growths,   grouped with Bourgeois Growths, they rank in the 1855 classification of the Gironde below the Great Growths and the Exceptional Growths

Astringency,   the dry feeling produced in the mouth, particularly at the sides of the tongue, caused by the high tannin content of young wines

Auslese, **owss***layzuh*

Ausone (Ch.), *ohzohn*

Bad Dürkheim, *bad* **deerk***hime*

Bad Kreuznach, *bad* **kroyts***nak*

Bagaçeira, *baga***say***ra*

Baked,   an adjective applied to the bouquet and aroma of wines originating in hot countries, which taste cooked and earthy

Barbera, *bar***bair***uh*

Barrique, *bareek*,   a Bordeaux hogshead, containing about 48 gallons (approximately 225 litres), yielding about 24 cases

Beaujolais, *bohzholay*

Beaune, Côte de, *koht de bohn*

Big,   a full-bodied, mouth-filling wine with plenty of alcohol and flavour

Bodega, *bo***day***guh*

Body,   describing the mouth-filling qualities of a wine

Bottle sizes,   One bottle contains 75 cl (Champagne 80 cl); one half bottle contains 37·5 cl (Champagne 40 cl). The Magnum equals two bottles, the Tappit-hen three bottles, the Jeroboam four bottles, the Rehoboam six bottles, and the Methuselah eight bottles. The Salmanezah (twelve bottles), Balthazar (sixteen bottles) and the Nebuchadnezzar (twenty bottles) are not now made

Bouquet, *bookay*,   the smell of

wine discovered by the nose

Bourgeois Growths, *boorzhwah*, see Artisan Growths

Bourgeuil, *boorguh-ee*

Brouillis, *brooyee*

Brut, *broo*

Bual, *booal*

Butt,   a Spanish cask (particularly of sherry) containing about 108 gallons (just under 500 litres), and yielding 51 to 53 cases

Cabernet Franc, *kaburnay fraw*

Cabernet-Sauvignon, *kaburnay-sohveenyaw*

Cacao, Crême de, *krem de kakow*

Calon-Ségur (Ch.) *kalahng-saygoor*

Cambium,   the extremely thin layer beneath the bark of a twig, branch or trunk, which must be joined between the stock and scion for a graft to succeed

Carignan, *kareenyaw*

Carton, Case,   the standard selling unit of wines and spirits, containing 12 bottles, 24 half bottles or 6 magnums, amounting to 9 litres. A carton of Bordeaux bottles weighs 22 kg (48 lbs) and measures $26 \times 39 \times 33$ cm ($10'' \times 15'' \times 13''$)

Chablis, *shablee*

Chai, *shay*

Chambolle-Musigny, *shombol-moozeeny*

Chardonnay, *shardonay*

Chassagne-Montrachet, *shassine-mawnrashay*

Chasselas, *shassuhlah*

Château, *shato*, literally *castle*, applied to a French mansion and to its vineyard. Abbreviated to 'Ch.' See also 'Domaine'

Châteauneuf-du-Pape, *shatohnuf-doo-pap*

Chenin Blanc, *shenan blaw*

Chianti, *keeanti*

Chinon, *sheenaw*

Cinsault, *sansoh*

Classico, **klas**seekoh

Climens (Ch.), *kleemaw*

Coaster,   a tray, sometimes on wheels, for holding a decanter or bottle, to be passed round a dining-table

Cognac, *konyak*

Cointreau, *kwahntroh*

Condrieu, *kondree-uh*

Corky,   a rotten, persistent smell, caused by a cork that has gone bad

Côte d'Or, *koht dor*

Coutet (Ch.), *kootay*

Criadera, *kreeadairuh*

Curaçao, *kyoorasoh*

Deidesheim, *die-des-hime*

Doisy-Daëne, *dwahzee-den*

Domaine, the Burgundian equivalent of a château

Dordogne, *dordoyn*

Doux, *doo*

Ducru-Beaucaillou (Ch.), *dookroo-bohkeye-yoo*

d'Yquem (Ch.), *deekem*

Eau-de-vie-de-marc, *ohduhveeduhmah*

Edelfäule, *aydelfoyluh*

Eiswein, *icevine*

Entre-deux-Mers, *awntruh-duh-mair*

Esters,   compounds of alcohols and organic acids which give flavour to wines and spirits

Exceptional Growths,   in the 1855 classification, these rank immediately below the Grands Crus of the Médoc. There are six, some of which deserve higher classification

Fat, a big, soft wine containing a high proportion of glycerine

Filhot (Ch.), *feelyoh*

Finos, *feenohs*

Framboise, *frawmbwahz*

Garganega, *garganayga*

Gay-Lussac, *gay-loossak*,   a French scientist who defined the process of fermentation chemically. The metric system of describing alcohol strength (% by volume) is named after him

Genever, *djenayver*,   Hollands gin

Gevrey-Chambertin, *zhevray-shawmbertan*

Gewürztraminer, *gevoortstrameener*

Grand Marnier, *graw marneeay*

Graves, *grahv*

Grenache, *grenahsh*

Grolleau (Groslot), *grohloh*

Guyot Double, *geeoh doobluh*

Haut-Médoc, *oh-maydok*

Hermitage, *ermeetahzh*

Hogshead,   a general term for a cask of about 50 gallons (225 litres), having different names and capacities in different regions. A hogshead of sherry equals half a butt, a hogshead of port equals half a pipe, a hogshead of brandy equals half a puncheon. See also 'Barrique' and 'Pièce'.

Hospices de Beaune, *ospeess de bohn*

Infusion, filtering hot or cold wine, spirit or water through a bed of flavouring herbs, as in making coffee

Jerez, *hereth*

Jura, *zhooruh*

Kiedrich, *keedrik*

Kirsch, *keersh*

Kümmel, *kimel*

Lafite (Ch.), *lafeet*

Léoville-Barton (Ch.), *layohveel-bartaw*

Lees,   sediment in the bottom of a cask, vat or bottle; eliminated by filtering, racking or decanting

Liebfraumilch, *leebfrowmilk*

Light,   light in body, as opposed to full-bodied

Lynch-Bages (Ch.), *lansh-bahzh*

Maceration, soaking flavouring herbs in hot or cold wine, spirit or water, as in making tea

Mâconnais, *makonay*

Maderized, 'like the wines of Madeira'; this is a libel on the name of a fine wine. Both wines have a 'burnt' flavour and a brown colour, but the flavour and colour of maderized wines are not clean, being caused by oxidasic degeneration through excessive exposure to light and air

Malbec, *malbek*

Malmsey, *mahmsay*

Manzanilla, *manza*nee*yuh*

Maraschino, *maraskee*noh

Marc, *mah*

Margaux (Ch.), *margoh*

Médoc, *maydok*

Merlot, *mairloh*

Meursault, *mersoh*

Midi, *meedee*

Mourvèdre, *moorvedruh*

Müller-Thurgau, *miller-toorgow*

Muscadet (Gamay Blanc), *mooskaday*

Muscat, *mooskah*

Nahe, *na-huh*

Niederhausen, **nee***derhowsen*

Nierstein, *neershtine*

Nuits, Côte de, *koht duh nwee*

Nuits St. George, *nwee san zhorzh*

Oestrich, *uhstrik*

Orvieto, *orvee***ay***toh*

Ouzo, *oozoh*

Oxidized, a burnt, raisiny smell and taste of wine that has been exposed to the air, perhaps through faulty storage. See also 'Maderized'

Pauillac, *poyyak*

Pedro Ximenes, *paydroh* hi**mayn**es

Periquita, *perikeeta*

Pétillant, *payteeyaw*, slightly sparkling; less than 1·5 atmosphere pressure

Picpoul, *pikpool*

Pièce, *pyess*, a Burgundy or Champagne hogshead of about 50 gallons (225 litres)

Pinot, *peenoh*

Pinot Gris, *peenoh gree*

Pinot Noir, *peenoh nwar*

Pipe, a cask, longer and thinner than the Spanish butt, containing 100 gallons (455 litres) approximately. A pipe of port or Tarragona holds 115 gallons (522 litres); a pipe of Madeira or Marsala holds 92 to 93 gallons (420 litres)

Pommard, *pommar*

Portacask, a shipping container made of fibreglass, lined with stainless steel, holding 580 gallons (26·4 Hl)

Pouilly-Fuissé, *pooyee-fweesay*

Pricked, acetic

Puligny-Montrachet, *pooleenyee-mawnrashay*

Puncheon, a cask. A puncheon of brandy holds 120 gallons (545 litres); a puncheon of rum is normally 93 gallons (422 litres), but varies considerably

Qualitätswein mit Prädikat, kvali*taytsvine mit* **pray***dikat*
Quinta, **keen***tah*

Rayas, **rye***as*
Rheingau, *ringehow*
Riesling, **reess***ling* (the most frequently mispronounced wine word!)
Rioja, *reeoka*
Robust, full-bodied, rich in alcohol and/or tannin. Such wines can stand travel well, but may need ageing to become palatable

Saar, *zah*
Safrap, a steel container lined with plastic, holding 535 gallons (24·4 Hl)
St. Emilion, *santaymeelyaw*
St. Julien, *sanzhoolyan*
Santenay, *sawntenay*
Saumur, *sohmoor*
Sauternes, *sohtern*
Schaumwein, *showmvine*
Schloss Böckelheim, *schloss buhrkelhime*
Sémillon, *saymeeyaw*
Sercial, *sersyal*
Soave, *soh-ahvay*
Spätlese, *shpaytlayzuh*
Suduiraut (Ch.), *soodeeroh*
Syrah, *seerah*

Tailles, *tie*
Tannins, phenolic substances occurring in the stalk, skin and pips of the grape (and in many other plants, especially the wood from which casks are made). Tannins help to preserve the wine and to clear it, besides influencing colour
Tart, excessively acid
Tokay, *tokeye*
Tonneau, *tonoh*, a selling measure amounting to four hogsheads (900 litres), yielding about 96 cases. There is no cask or vat of this name

Ugni Blanc, *oonyee blaw*
Urzig, *oortsik*

Valpolicella, *valpoli***chel***la*
Verdelho, *vair***day***lyoh*
Verdicchio, *ver***deek***yoh*
Vigneron, *veenyeraw*
Vin de Goutte, *van de goot*
Vin (Rouge, Blanc, Rosé), *van roozh, van blaw, van rohzay*, wines without any distinguishing *appellation*. These *vins ordinaires* can be excellent. Eighty per cent of all wines consumed are of this order. The 1914 soldier's pronunciation of 'vin blanc' originated the term 'plonk'
Vinhos Verdes, *veenyoosh vairdsh*
Vosne-Romanée, *vohn-rohmanay*
Vougeot, *voozhoh*
Vouvray, *voovray*

Wehlen, *vaylen*
Winkel, *vingkel*
Worms, *voorms*

Index